1846–86

COMBAT

Apache Warrior VERSUS US Cavalryman

Sean McLachlan

Illustrated by Adam Hook

First published in Great Britain in 2016 by Osprey Publishing,
PO Box 883, Oxford, OX1 9PL, UK
1385 Broadway, 5th Floor, New York, NY 10018, USA
E-mail: info@ospreypublishing.com

Osprey Publishing, part of Bloomsbury Publishing Plc

A CIP catalog record for this book is available from the British Library

Print ISBN: 978 1 4728 1246 9
PDF ebook ISBN: 978 1 4728 1247 6
ePub ebook ISBN: 978 1 4728 1248 3

Index by Rob Munro
Typeset in Univers, Sabon, and Adobe Garamond Pro
Maps by bounford.com
Originated by PDQ Media, Bungay, UK
Printed in China through World Print Ltd.

16 17 18 19 20 10 9 8 7 6 5 4 3 2 1

www.ospreypublishing.com

Key to military symbols

XXXXX Army Group, XXXX Army, XXX Corps, XX Division, X Brigade, III Regiment, II Battalion, I Company/Battery, ●●● Platoon, ●● Section, ● Squad, Infantry, Artillery, Cavalry, Airborne, Unit HQ, Air defence, Air Force, Air mobile, Air transportable, Amphibious, Anti-tank, Armour, Air aviation, Bridging, Engineer, Headquarters, Maintenance, Medical, Missile, Mountain, Navy, Nuclear, biological, chemical, Ordnance, Parachute, Reconnaissance, Signal, Supply, Transport movement, Fortress or static, MG Fortress machine gun

Key to unit identification

Unit identifier, Parent unit, Commander, (+) with added elements, (–) less elements

Dedication

To Almudena, my wife, and Julián, my son.

Acknowledgments

Several experts were consulted in the preparation of this book. I would especially like to thank Alvin R. Lynn for answering many questions about the First Battle of Adobe Walls. Archaeologist Skip Keith Miller shared his findings from the battle of Cieneguilla site. Fellow Osprey writer and author of *U.S. Dragoons 1833–55* John Langellier helped me unravel the mysteries of the Dragoon uniform. I would also like to thank Dr. Ellen B. Basso and Dr. Peter M. Gardner for firing my interest in cultural anthropology.

Artist's note

Readers may care to note that the original paintings from which the artwork plates in this book were prepared are available for private sale. All reproduction copyright whatsoever is retained by the Publishers. All inquiries should be addressed to:

Scorpio, 158 Mill Road, Hailsham, East Sussex BN27 2SH, UK
Email: scorpiopaintings@btinternet.com

The Publishers regret that they can enter into no correspondence upon this matter.

Editor's note

US customary measurements are used in this book. For ease of comparison please refer to the following conversion table:

1 mile = 1.6km
1yd = 0.9m
1ft = 0.3m
1in = 2.54cm/25.4mm
1lb = 0.45kg

CONTENTS

Introduction

When the United States defeated Mexico in 1848, it captured a great swath of the country – what is now California, New Mexico, Arizona, Nevada, Utah, and parts of Wyoming and Colorado; a total of some 525,000 square miles. This gave the young nation room to expand and a huge potential for agriculture, ranching, and mineral prospecting in areas still largely unexplored. It also brought the United States into conflict with the original inhabitants of that region. Many of the tribes had been hostile to the Mexicans and soon grew angry at the influx of American settlers who took their traditional lands. The most hostile group, and the one that resisted the longest, was the Apache.

It is unclear when the Apache moved into the American Southwest, what is now Arizona, New Mexico, and western Texas. They were fully settled there by the time the first Spanish explorers came to the region in the mid-16th century, and may have been there for centuries before that. The scattered bands survived by hunting and gathering, as well as raiding the more settled tribes. They had a fiercely independent streak and developed a bitter hatred for the Mexicans, who tried to exterminate them and even offered official government bounties for Apache scalps – 100 pesos for the scalp of males aged 14 or over, 50 for a female scalp, and 25 for that of a child.

Coyotero Apache scouts at Apache Lake, Sierra Blanca Mountains, Arizona, 1873. The lush uplands of Arizona are "sky islands" of greenery and readily available water scattered about the harsh desert. It was prime land for Apache and settler alike, and many of the battles in the Apache Wars occurred as fights over this land. (LoC)

The Apache had been largely successful in maintaining their independence from the Spanish *conquistadores* and later the Mexican Army. The newcomers were too few in number and too poorly equipped to do more than protect their walled villages and the surrounding farmland. Sometimes they weren't even capable of that. The Spanish and Mexicans did, however, inflict losses on the Apache, losses the small bands could ill afford to sustain.

At first the Apache were neutral toward the Americans, but their natural suspicions were soon confirmed by the actions of dishonest traders and the influx of immigrants who took their land with no thought as to who had been there before. Raids by young warriors on American settlements led to reprisals by civilian vigilantes and the American armed forces. Peace talks led nowhere, for American negotiators didn't understand that a chief lacked full authority. The chief would sign a peace agreement with the full intent of trying to control his warriors, but he couldn't enforce his will even on his own band, let alone all the others. So when there was another raid, the Americans would feel the chief had tricked them. The chief, on the other hand, would feel the Americans were blaming him for matters beyond his control.

An Apache band, probably an extended family, in front of their wickiups, near Camp Apache, Arizona, 1873. These brush shelters covered with hides or cloth were quick to make. As one Apache remembered, they were "rather primitive as compared to the tents of the prairie tribes and certainly far less advanced than the adobe dwellings of the Pueblo Indians. It was, however, well adapted to our wandering kind of life and especially to the fact that we frequently had to move in a great hurry and to abandon our camps to our enemies" (quoted in Betzinez & Nye 1959: 29). Reservations were one technique for breaking Apache independence. Camp Apache had been founded as a reservation the year before. It was consolidated into the San Carlos Agency in 1876 when that agency assumed responsibility for the entire White Mountain Reservation. Camp Apache was renamed Fort Apache in 1879. The land is still a reservation today. (LoC)

Tensions soon escalated into a state of constant conflict. To call this a war would be misleading, as there was only one nation-state involved in fighting a host of independent groups that at any one time ranged from openly hostile to fully cooperative. Violence rose and fell, with cooler heads on both sides trying to find a solution but having their efforts hampered by eager young warriors, vigilantes, and inexperienced officers who thought any Apache was a bad Apache.

The fighting saw the confrontation of two very different styles of combat. On the one side, there were the Apache warriors. Brave, strong, intimately familiar with the terrain, and capable of almost superhuman feats of endurance, they were masters of hit-and-run warfare. Knowing they could not face the US Cavalry in open battle, they chose to fight the way they had always fought, with lightning raids followed by swift withdrawal into the rough mountain chains that crisscross the region. They compensated for their inferior weaponry and scarce ammunition by picking away at enemy units and exhausting them by leading them on long chases through harsh terrain.

The US Cavalry went through several important changes during this period, many of them prompted by its lack of success against the Apache. At the beginning of our period, the US Dragoons were undermanned and poorly armed and equipped. Nevertheless, they carried the fight to the Apache and did the best they could. Later cavalry units received better armament and reinforcements. More importantly, they gained experience. Wagons were replaced by mules, and inefficient and unreliable scouts were replaced by loyal Apache scouts. Weapons were improved, uniforms were adapted to better suit the climate, and the men became hardened to the rigors of fighting in the American Southwest.

HARPER'S WEEKLY.
A JOURNAL OF CIVILIZATION.

Vol. XXXIII.—No. 1686.
Copyright, 1889, by Harper & Brothers.
All Rights Reserved.

NEW YORK, SATURDAY, APRIL 13, 1889.

TEN CENTS A COPY.
WITH A SUPPLEMENT.

THE FRONTIER TROOPER'S THANATOPSIS.—From the Painting by Frederic Remington.—[See Page 282.]

This print from *Harper's Weekly*, titled "The Frontier trooper's thanatopsis," dates to 1889 and was the work of Frederic Remington. The burial scaffold in the background shows this was obviously done on the Great Plains, since that was the funeral custom of many Plains tribes, but the uniform is accurate for the period. (LoC)

The Apache were learning too. They took advantage of the international border to flee from one side to the other, they played upon some American officers' overconfidence and assumption of Apache inferiority, and they acquired the latest weapons by any means they could. The result was a hard fight lasting decades, a life-and-death struggle set against the punishing but beautiful backdrop of the American Southwest.

Apacheria

The area where the US Cavalry fought the Apache was divided into various military departments that changed over time. This map shows the operational area in the 1870s and 1880s, at the height of the fighting.

The independent Republic of Texas was admitted as a state in 1845, one of the main factors that led to the Mexican–American War. In 1850–63 the present-day states of Arizona and New Mexico formed one territory called the New Mexico Territory. In 1863 they were divided along their modern lines and became the Arizona and New Mexico territories; both would become states in 1912.

The period 1866–91 was that of greatest stability, and the departmental boundaries did not change. During that time the Military Division of the Missouri oversaw much of the American West. It had various regional departments from the Rio Grande to the Canadian border, and it had two departments that were concerned with the Apache: the Department of Texas ran most of that state, while the Department of the Missouri was responsible for the northern Texas Panhandle, New Mexico Territory, the Indian Territory, Colorado Territory, Kansas, Missouri, and Illinois. West of this was the Military Division of the Pacific. During 1870–93, southern California and Arizona Territory were in its Department of Arizona.

Insights as to how this territory was administered are provided by a brief exploration of the organization of troops in the Territory of New Mexico in 1876. It is striking just how few men guarded this large territory – only a little over 1,000 officers and men for 121,589 square miles of mountains and desert. They were based in only eight forts, five of which were in Apache lands. Four of those five forts had cavalry companies. Most forts throughout the territory had both infantry and cavalry companies, but this was a cost-cutting measure. While infantry could not hope to keep up with the swift Apache, they were much cheaper to maintain and could perform garrison duty, guard reservations and settlements, and undertake limited patrolling.

Cavalry did the "heavy lifting" in the Apache Wars, following the Apache into their strongholds. Often these long chases led them into other departments and even other divisions. Cavalry from New Mexico often chased Apache into Arizona and vice versa. In general, this was not a problem other than bureaucratic wrangling about who had to pay for the refitting of a cavalry company stopping in a fort not their own. Local officers generally let the officer in charge of the column retain command unless there was a need for an overall commander, as was the case on various large-scale hunts for renegades such as after the battle of Cibecue Creek and during the Geronimo campaign.

Conversely, the boundaries of the various tribes of Apache were fluid and constantly changing. As hunter-gatherer-raiders, they did not have firm boundaries and individual bands often moved across these blurred lines.

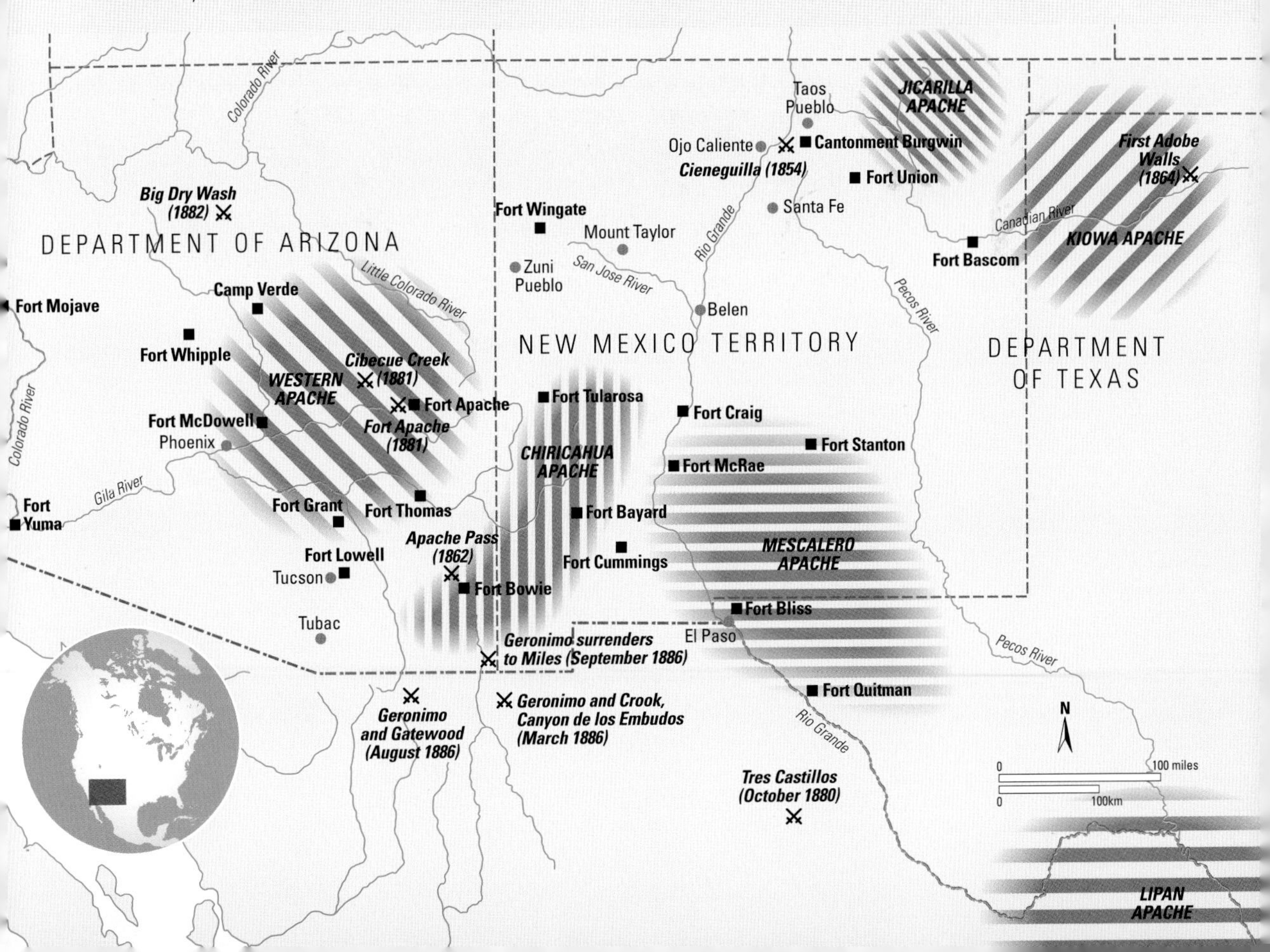

The Opposing Sides

MOTIVATION AND MORALE

Apache

The term "Apache" is vague at best. It is not a word used by the people themselves, but means "the feared enemy" in the language of the Zuni people. "Apache" is applied to a number of nomadic or semi-nomadic groups of Athabascan speakers in the American Southwest. These groups referred to themselves using variations on the words *ne dene*, which means "the people."

The Apache only considered themselves one people in the most general sense, although that sense of identity increased in the face of encroaching enemies. Apache groups often fought each other, and there was virtually no political organization above the band. A "chief" was simply the most respected person in one band or *rancheria*, the small temporary settlements the Apache would make. Those who didn't agree with a chief were free to leave; and as is common with nomadic peoples, bands often split for personal or practical reasons.

The Apache man's life focused on hunting and war. He considered manual labor beneath him and left it to the women. Only the heaviest manual labor and tasks related to the hunt and raid, such as caring for horses, was done by men. As Joseph Hoffman, an Apache who grew up in the 1860s, recalled: "About all that we did in those days was to hunt and fight" (quoted in Basso 1971: 79).

The Apache saw warfare differently from Mexicans and Americans, who used war to completely defeat an enemy and gain political and territorial victory. James Kaywaykla, a Warm Springs Apache who was born in 1877, stated: "Until I was about ten years old I did not know that people died except by violence. That is because I am an Apache, a Warm Springs Apache, whose first vivid memories are of being driven from our reservation near Ojo Caliente with fire and sword" (Ball & Kaywaykla 1970: 13). For the Apache, warfare was about raiding – sometimes to settle scores in feuds, but

An Apache ambush is depicted in this work by Edward Vebell. The US Cavalry are galloping into a narrow canyon, no doubt in pursuit of some bait in the form of a few Apache warriors or women. For the sake of the painting's composition, the artist has placed the Apache in a position that they never would have taken. The men would be lying prone, not standing, and a younger warrior would be holding the horses well out of sight. Bands took along young men who had not yet reached full maturity to do menial tasks such as cooking and caring for horses. These apprentice warriors would observe the fights and learn from their elders. (Illustration by Ed Vebell/Getty Images)

more often for the sake of plunder. Thus the Apache would only fight if reasonably sure of victory, and would retreat quickly if the stakes became too high. When backed into a corner, however, they would fight fiercely no matter what the odds.

An essential piece of Apache kit was the yellow pollen of the *tule*, a general term for several types of cattail rushes and similar plants found along the banks of streams. Called *hoddentin* in Apache, this pollen had a deep religious significance, symbolizing health, growth, and vitality. It was carried in a small sack, usually on the ammunition belt. Before going after his enemies, the Apache warrior would throw a pinch of this powder at the sun, and then put a pinch on his tongue and forehead. Just before a raid, pinches of *hoddentin* were offered to the rising sun and the four directions to guarantee a safe return. It was also said to heal the sick or weary if ingested. A medicine man would walk in front of a wounded member of the party throwing pinches of *hoddentin* to help him on his way. This pollen was used in virtually all Chiricahua ceremonies to bless and purify people.

US Cavalry

The men of the US Cavalry came from a variety of backgrounds and joined for many reasons. Some were typical of men going to war throughout history – the search for adventure; fleeing poverty, boredom, or the law; and the chance for personal advancement. There was an additional factor: the Desert

A cavalry patrol departs from Fort Bowie. (Photo by Time Life Pictures/US Signal Corps/ The LIFE Picture Collection/ Getty Images)

Southwest was a frontier full of opportunity. Once they finished their service, many soldiers used their savings to start businesses or buy land. Old West history is full of stories of soldiers who went on to become leaders in civilian life. Having spent several years in the service, they could certainly be said to have earned it.

Many of the troops who fought against the Apache were from African-American units – a fact ignored by novels, Hollywood, and even some history books. The 9th and 10th Cavalry, and the 24th and 25th Infantry, were composed of black troops under the command of white officers. African-Americans were treated as second-class citizens in Army as well as civilian life. While paid the same as their white counterparts, they received inferior equipment and horses. They have also been treated as second-class citizens by early historians: many books written in the first half of the 20th century talk about the exploits of these regiments without mentioning they were black. A casual reader in that period could have been forgiven for thinking that the pacifying of Apacheria was entirely undertaken by white people.

Surgeon George Henry Roberts Moran kept a diary in 1878 while stationed at Camp Bowie and Camp Thomas in Arizona. He records vaccinating troops, the boredom of camp life, shooting rattlesnakes, and a fellow officer discovering a tarantula in his bed. In March of 1878, at Camp Bowie, he recorded the following cases: "1 for Typho-Malarial Fever; 1 Acute Dysentary; 4 Primary Syphillis; 1 Constitutional Syphillis; 1 Inebriation;

2 Acute Rheumatism; 2 Boil, etc." (quoted in Moran & Hagemann 1963: 258). One wonders what agonies were hidden under the label "etc."

Desertion rates in the US Cavalry were sometimes as high as 40 percent annually. Given the terrain, it was easy to desert and hard for undermanned outposts to track down the deserters. Settlers were generally sympathetic to deserters, and the proximity of the border tempted many. Interestingly, the rate of desertion among black troops was considerably lower, perhaps because they were more accustomed to hardship in their daily lives. In 1885, the reward for catching a deserter rose from $30 to $100. Laws were passed making aiding, abetting, or harboring deserters a federal crime. If caught, punishment was severe. The deserter would be dishonorably discharged, forfeit his pay, have his head shaved, and the letter "D" branded on his left hip.

Wearing sharpshooter collar insignia, this Buffalo Soldier of Company D, 9th Cavalry was photographed at some point in time between 1880 and 1890. (LoC)

MOBILITY AND LOGISTICS

Apache

The Apache had an inherent advantage over the Army and settlers. While the Apache roved the countryside, the whites stayed in one place, thus suffering the tactical disadvantage of being isolated in a known position. Long supply lines, slow communications, and easily cut telegraph wires also worked to the whites' disadvantage. While fighting Brigadier General George Crook, the Apache often cut the telegraph wire and put in a splice of wet rawhide. When the rawhide dried it was almost indistinguishable from the copper wire itself, and repair crews took ages to find the damage. Copper wire became a fashionable ornament for Apache women.

The US Cavalry couldn't keep up with the swift-riding Apache, who would bring along several mounts per man and ride one to exhaustion before mounting another. The exhausted horse was eaten, something the cavalry wouldn't do. It was common for the Apache to ride 100 miles in a day even on rough terrain. Knowing they were being tracked, the Apache hid their passage by leaping from rock to rock or following streams. Some regions of Arizona have large lava fields left by now-extinct volcanoes. These can be crossed without leaving a trace. Palmer Valor, an Apache warrior, remembered a raid into Mexico:

> There was a big bunch of us, but we didn't travel all together. That's the way we used to do—two or three, or maybe five, or anywhere up to eleven of us would get together to go to Mexico ... [we] came to a dangerous spot where we had to walk

Apache warrior

The Apache went on campaign with a minimum of equipment, preferring to move lightly and quickly while living off the land. This warrior came to Cibecue Creek knowing he would attack the cavalry and then head out into the wilderness, so he arrived ready for an extended campaign.

Cibecue Creek, August 30, 1881

Weapons, dress, and equipment

His primary weapon is a Winchester Model 1873 short rifle (**1**). The "gun that won the West" became hugely popular and soon made its way into Apache hands. Apache sometimes donned a variety of western clothing, but stripped down to the basics when fighting. Headgear was not a traditional part of the Apache wardrobe, but men often wore hats they had acquired in battle or purchased. This man wears new moccasins (**2**). These reached about halfway to the knee and had a thick rawhide sole as well as a turned-up, reinforced toe. As anyone who has hiked in the American Southwest can attest, thick boots are essential for protecting the feet from sharp stones, cacti, and rattlesnakes. He carries extra buckskin and soles (**3**) tucked into the waistband of his breechclout. The long marches the Apaches endured made spares essential. The overhanging fold of the moccasin uppers could be used as pockets, as this warrior is doing with a needle made of a mescal thorn and thread made of deer sinew (**4**).

On his belt is a small satchel of *hoddentin* (**5**), the sacred pollen of the cattail plant. Rifle rounds are carried on a cartridge belt the warrior made himself (**6**), which also holds a sheathed knife (**7**). As a backup weapon and for hunting, he carries a bow in a protective leather case (**8**) with an extra bowstring. His quiver (**9**) contains 18 arrows.

Young Apache warrior and woman near Camp Apache, Arizona, 1873. The warrior carries a quiver slung over his back and holds a pair of arrows. The woman carries a load on her back supported by a forehead strap. The Apache were accustomed to carrying heavy loads over long distances – something that would stand them in good stead in their fights against the US Cavalry. (LoC)

> on our toes to be sure that we left no tracks and be sure that we hid all our tracks. This place is a great plain, all open, and if the Mexicans had ever found our tracks on it, they could have run us down for sure because we were all on foot. There is only one mountain on this plain, and it is so far from any other mountain where we could have taken cover that we could have easily been caught. (Quoted in Basso 1971: 47)

OPPOSITE Apache at a ford in a river, photographed by the famous Western photographer Edward Curtis, *c.*1903. Given the bare foliage and the blankets wrapped around the men, it appears to be winter. The weather can get quite cold in the American Southwest, especially in the uplands, and it was a tactic of the US Cavalry to burn all shelter and destroy any blankets or clothing they came upon, thereby adding to Apache misery and eroding their morale. (LoC)

Sometimes the Apache left a trail to lead pursuers into an ambush. In one case, an Apache woman left a trail that was a bit too clear, and the cavalry in pursuit grew suspicious, especially when they noticed she deliberately avoided rocky areas that could have hidden her tracks. In another case in the Black Mountain Range, when a band had stolen some horses, a group of 20 civilians went after them. The posse saw three of the missing horses, but when they approached the horses they found themselves in an ambush. Six of the civilians were killed before the rest could escape.

Another popular Apache trick was to flee across the border. The US Cavalry often chased them into Mexico and even scouted there, although for most of this period they weren't supposed to. Even in periods when both nations had an accord to allow cavalry in hot pursuit to cross the line, it was a tricky endeavor due to lingering resentments over the Mexican–American

An Apache and his wife, 1873. Both appear to have come into town for trading and are well dressed for the occasion. Note how bedraggled their horse is. While the Apache tried to take good care of their mounts, they did not always have the means to do so, what with chronic shortage of food and forage, plus long rides in search of safe refuges away from the US Cavalry. (LoC)

War and outlaws like the Cowboys of Tombstone fame rustling cattle south of the border. The Apache, of course, had no such compunction. This attitude remains among Native Americans. One member of the Tohono O'odham tribe, whose traditional lands straddle the Mexico–US border, told the author that his relations in Mexico often came up to the United States to work. He saw nothing wrong with this since his people pre-dated the border and laughed at the concept that a Native American could be an "illegal immigrant."

The Apache were eager to get firearms. While selling guns to the Indians was illegal, there were always people willing to circumvent the law for quick cash. These sources were uncertain and costly, so the Apache supplemented their firepower with captured arms and often raids were launched specifically to procure weapons. Since selling bullets to the Indians was also illegal, the Apache became adept at casting their own. Lead being scarce in the region, silver and even gold were used, and there are reports of Apache carving bullets out of stone. Gunpowder was always in short supply and often old or of poor quality, for those who sold armaments to the Apache were not above selling inferior merchandise. Because of the chronic shortage of guns and powder, many warriors continued to carry simpler weapons.

The Apache were masters at using terrain to their advantage because their itinerant lifestyle gave them a deep knowledge of the land. They knew the best places for an ambush or hideout, and where to find game and water. They did not use much camouflage, although there are some reports of warriors tying plants around their heads in order to blend into the landscape. More often, they simply used the rough terrain for cover. The glare of the harsh desert sun on the rocks, and the deep shadows the sun casts between them, are often enough to hide a man from view. Cavalrymen remarked that they could pass so close to a hidden Apache that the man could almost reach out and touch him, yet he remained invisible.

US Cavalry

The US Cavalry found itself in a harsh environment chasing an elusive foe. When the United States took over the Southwest region, large portions of it weren't even mapped. In the early years, the undermanned garrisons were often quite literally heading off into the unknown. As one unnamed officer of Troop B, 4th Cavalry, recalled in the *Saturday Globe* of Utica, New York on October 25, 1902:

> I served all through the latter part of the Geronimo campaign under Gen. [H.W.] Lawton [commander of B Troop, 4th Cavalry], who was then a colonel [*sic*; Lawton was a captain at the time]. We were out six months and during that entire period not one of us had a change of clothing. The campaigning was through one of the most mountainous countries in the world. Sometimes we would climb up the side of an almost perpendicular slope and at other times the descent was so steep that we were obliged to let our horses down over ledges of rocks by lariats tied to their tails.

The Cavalry favored heavy western horse breeds for their endurance and strength. Speed wasn't a main concern, because the land was considered to be too rough and treacherous to risk galloping in most places. In contrast to the Apache, cavalrymen tried to rest their animals as much as possible. A horse would generally carry about 240lb of weapons, ammunition, and gear, so men

Fort Thomas, 1876. This photograph gives a good idea of the remote and desolate nature of most forts in Apacheria. It also shows how the forts were open and unfortified, the soldiers being confident that the Apache would not attack a well-armed settlement. Food was of poor quality and monotonous. The meat ration was three-tenths bacon and seven-tenths fresh beef. Bread was baked at the post bakery, but soon ran out on long patrols. Beans thickened with cornstarch were a staple. Fruit and vegetables were luxuries, with the result that many men developed scurvy. In his 1884 report, Brigadier General George Crook complained: "This question of food is in Arizona of grave consequence. Military posts are from a variety of causes often prevented from maintaining vegetable gardens and the soldier must consequently look more and more to his superiors for good, wholesome rations; a failure to supply these will often breed discontent, the logical sequence to which is always inefficient service or desertion." Posts in more moderate climates planted gardens; but as Crook mentioned, this wasn't always possible, and often posts would be so undermanned there wasn't time to tend a garden. In another part of the report, Crook has to repeat a request made several times by his cartographer for $375 for mapmaking materials. That at such a late date he had to haggle over such a modest sum in order to create much-needed maps says a great deal about federal parsimony at this time. (Arizona Historical Society, #25613)

COMBAT Private, 6th Cavalry

This private from Company D, 6th Cavalry, has just come from Fort Apache so his kit is in better shape than that of his comrades on extended campaign, who often returned literally in rags. Even so, his uniform is faded from the sun and shows numerous repairs where it was caught by thorns and sharp rocks.

Cibecue Creek, August 30, 1881

Weapons, dress, and equipment

He carries a .45-70 Springfield Model 1877 "Trapdoor" carbine (**1**). The carbine's metal would have initially been blued, but this caught the light and exposed the shooter's position, so the men always dulled the metal. He has left his bayonet at home – as early as the Civil War, troopers had decided this appendage was only useful as a tent peg! His other weapon is a .45 caliber Colt Model 1873 Single Action Army revolver. This six-shooter was hugely popular on the frontier for both civilian and military use.

His notoriously fragile black campaign hat (**2**) has lost its shape. His Model 1872 half-boots (**3**) are well suited for the environment, and give more protection than the brogans and bootees they replaced. The Colt's holster (**4**) is Civil War surplus, which were only just being used up by this time. He wears a homemade cartridge belt (**5**) for the pistol ammunition. These belts were popular because they offered easier access to the cartridges, although they were exposed to the elements. On his left side is a Model 1880 hunting knife (**6**) and scabbard, the knife doubling as an entrenching tool.

Brigadier General Crook on his mule "Apache" accompanied by two Apache scouts, Dutchy and Alchesay. When Crook took over the Department of Arizona in 1871, he brought with him years of experience using mule trains against hostile natives in Nevada, Oregon, and Idaho. Mules could go where wagons could not. It was common for mule trains to travel up to 30 miles a day, although in rough terrain it could be half that. Much greater distances are recorded. In 1882, a company of Apache scouts chasing the Loco outbreak from the San Carlos Agency in Arizona took a pack train with each animal loaded with 200lb on a forced march of 280 miles in just three days. In normal marches, each mule could carry 250lb and survive off the land. This greatly lessened the supply problems at the far-flung forts. Crook so favored the mule that he rode one instead of a horse. (Arizona Historical Society, #25625)

were recruited who weighed no more than 150lb. In his 1884 report to Secretary of War Robert Todd Lincoln, Crook bemoans the low quality of government horses. Of the latest shipment of 40 horses, he reported that

> one "bucked" itself to death, one died of an obscure disease, one gave out on the road, and sixteen others have been condemned by a board of survey ... It is a useless waste of money to buy such horses, not to mention the injustice to the soldier to compel him to ride them. It has been reported to me by regimental commanders that men have deserted rather than incur the risks of riding and managing them.

It wasn't until 1864, with the adoption of the *Cooke's Tactics* system, that frontier cavalry had a set of tactics designed especially for them. Its author, Colonel Phillip St. George Cooke of the 2nd Cavalry, included several tips for campaigning in the Desert Southwest. For example, he advocated that long expeditions should start with only 15 miles a day to train the horses, after which they could do 25. Marching in columns of fours reduced dust and helped to prevent localized delays from holding up the entire force. There should be halts of 2–5 minutes every hour, with the mounts encouraged to graze. At around noon there should be a "watering call" of 20–45 minutes, when the mounts could be watered.

Cooke encouraged the cavalry to trot for part of the day. This awakened the men and exercised different muscles, thus reducing strain. It also got the men and their horses to camp quicker, allowing for a longer period for rest and grazing. Cooke also suggested camp should be made early. While it was still light, the horses could be grazed farther away and brought in close at nightfall, where they could be watched as they grazed on grass in the immediate vicinity.

Cooke's manual was replaced in 1873 with *Upton's Tactics* by Lieutenant Colonel Emory Upton, 1st Artillery. Upton's manual, which remained in use until 1891, added new suggestions such as not having reveille sounded on the march before daylight, as horses rest better from midnight to dawn. He suggested small commands ride in columns of twos and that there should be 40–50yd between companies to reduce the chances of delays rippling down the line. On long

Lieutenant Charles Gatewood and Apache scouts fought against both Victorio and Geronimo, and Gatewood was crucial in the negotiations that finally convinced Geronimo to surrender. Brigadier General Crook's biggest innovation was mustering Apache scouts. Crook had a deep understanding and respect for Apache culture and realized Apache were highly individualistic. It was easy to find bored reservation Apache willing to go on the warpath against other bands for whom they had no sympathy. Scouts signed on for six months and were given uniforms that they cast aside when in battle in favor of the usual breechclouts and moccasins. They wore a red bandanna so the white soldiers wouldn't mistake them for hostiles. The experiment worked wonders. The scouts were expert trackers, eager to fight, and knew all the Apache tricks. They did chafe under Army discipline, however, and sometimes used their position to further personal vendettas. The soldiers also suspected them of leading the column away from bands with whom they had sympathy, but it is difficult to prove these allegations. In time, though, the troops appreciated their efficacy. So did renegade Apache as they found cavalry columns being led to their secret hiding spots by scouts who knew the terrain as well as any warrior. (Arizona Historical Society #19763)

marches the men should dismount and lead their mounts for 20–40 minutes every second or third hour, and always lead their mounts over steep ground, especially downhill.

In practice, scouting missions were grueling and often fruitless. For example, on March 17, 1878, First Lieutenant John A. Rucker arrived in Camp Bowie with 35 Indian scouts from Company C and 16 soldiers from companies H and L, 6th Cavalry, after a long scouting mission that saw them ride 450 miles while finding no hostiles. Constant patrolling in harsh conditions took its toll on men and equipment, as this letter from McMullins Station, Arizona Territory, dated September 10, 1872, attests:

> Here the thermometer has been standing at 100 and 102 and the breeze we get feels like the hot air from a furnace. I can't see any use in the government sending troops here to protect so miserable a country at such an enormous expense-better let the Indians have it ... Further, thing that makes it bad is the scarcity of water. Can not get enough to wash our faces and hardly sufficient to drink. That we do get is as muddy as any you will find in a mud puddle on the roadside. This place where I am staying is a little mud hut where everyone is obliged to stop in order to get water as there is no other watering place within 30 miles. The water here is drawn from a well 200 feet deep by means of mule, pulleys, etc. Tis considered good water here. You would not think it fit to drink. Tis very alkali and the more I drink of it the more thirsty I get. (Quoted in Gressley & Porter 1958: 36)

WEAPONS

Apache

Traditional weapons were simple: clubs, spears, and bows. Stone or flint was the most common material for the heads of clubs and spears, although the Apache did make use of metal when they could. Spears were often tipped with a saber looted from a dead enemy. Machetes and axes made of metal became a trade item in the Spanish period and were used both as tools and weapons. War clubs were typically a spherical stone attached to a wooden shaft.

The most common ranged weapon was the bow, made from tough, flexible mulberry wood and strung with animal sinew. Warriors carried an extra bowstring and sometimes a second bow. The arrows were of cane fletched with eagle or hawk feathers and measured 24–29in. Arrowheads were traditionally made of flint or obsidian, but metal arrowheads became common in the Spanish era. War arrows could be barbed, making them harder to remove from wounds. (Army surgeons carried a metal wire with a loop on the end that they would push into the wound in order to fish for the point.) Another trick was to fletch the arrows in such a way that there would be no spin in flight. War arrows would be horizontal in relation to the notch at the end of the arrow that fit onto the bowstring. Hunting arrows would be vertical in relation to the notch. Thus a war arrow could pass between the horizontal ribs of a human, while a hunting arrow passed between the vertical ribs of an animal. Apache warriors often aimed for the soft abdomen, and when Mexicans fought the Apache, some wrapped a blanket around their midriff as a crude form of armor.

Slow-acting poison was made from snake or spider venom, plant compounds, or even the juices from the decaying gall bladder of a deer. Joseph Hoffman relates:

> Our people used to use poison on their arrows, both in war and in hunting. This poison was made from a deer's spleen. This was dried first, then ground up fine and mixed in with the ground roots or stalk of nettles and also some plant which has a burning taste, like chili. The mixture is put all in a little sack made from a part of the deer's big intestine.
>
> Then when all is ready, the maker spits into the bag and ties it up tightly and quickly so that none of the bad air will escape. The bag is hung from a tree for about three to five days till good and rotten and in liquid form. Then it is taken out and painted on the points of arrows.
>
> If the poison gets dry and hard it can be ground up and mixed on a stone with spit, just as paint is.
>
> This is bad poison, and if you just have a scratch and get this in it, you will swell up all over. (Quoted in Basso 1971: 231)

In the days before antibiotics, blood poisoning was a death sentence. There are some reports of coating musket balls with this substance.

Uncertainty in supply meant the Apache carried a variety of firearms. Several Apache and cavalry sources mention pistols, but these were never traded for, only captured. The Apache preferred to fight from long range and thus pistols were of little use. On the other hand, the Apache were too

OPPOSITE Entitled "Apache chiefs Garfield, Puche Te Foya and Sanches," this colorized print shows the three named men as they pose together in ceremonial attire, two with bows in hand and all three in feathered headdress, 1899. The image, from an original W. Henry Jackson photograph, was published by the Detroit Photographic Company. Even in the later battles there are reports of warriors using bows. This weapon had the added benefit of silence, and could also be used for hunting on the march without making unwanted noise. (Photo by Transcendental Graphics/ Getty Images)

An unidentified warrior in a studio portrait, *c.*1880. Bows had an effective range of about 150yd, inferior to most early muskets, and if the Apache didn't have the element of surprise they often found themselves being picked off at long range. On the other hand, the bow could fire four to ten times for every shot from a flintlock and carried tremendous force. There are reports of arrows passing right through a warhorse and embedding into the ground on the other side. The Apache, having learned to hunt from an early age, were expert archers. Army surgeons noted that it was rare to treat a man for only a single arrow wound. Once hit, the disabled man would generally be hit again and again in rapid succession. (Photo by Transcendental Graphics/ Getty Images)

practical to discard any gun that came into their possession, so pistols were often given to youngsters to improve their skill. Shotguns captured from settlers were used for hunting but not for war due to their poor range. For much of the period covered here the Apache had muskets or rifles that were often a generation out of date, although at times they would have the latest in firepower, captured from enemies or illegally traded for. By the 1870s, the Apache had been at war long enough that they had captured a great deal of the latest weaponry, and US cavalryman Captain John Bourke relates that most adult men had Winchester or Springfield breechloaders.

Apache braves ready for the trail, near Camp Apache, Arizona, 1873. Two of the men have stripped down to breechclout and moccasins, this being the standard garb for fighting. American and Mexican clothing was popular for daily use, as can be seen by the man wearing the hat and the white shirt worn by another Apache, but this sort of clothing would be set aside before a fight as it increased the wearer's visibility. Two of the Apache carry Springfield muskets. The main firearm for both sides in the Civil War, huge numbers of these weapons circulated after the war and many ended up in Native American hands. (LoC)

US Cavalry

The weapons used by the US Cavalry changed several times over the course of the Apache Wars. Cavalry were issued with a saber, but though this looked impressive on parade, it had little use in the field. Most accounts say the saber was left in barracks, along with the bayonet issued with the carbine.

During the 1840s and 1850s, the US Dragoons were armed with the .69-caliber Springfield Model 1847 musketoon and the .54-caliber Springfield Model 1842 "horse pistol." The musketoon was often loaded with "buck and ball" by adding three .31-caliber balls along with the .69-caliber bullet. It was an unpopular weapon, having an effective range of less than 60yd. In 1854 the Inspector General of the US Army, Colonel Joseph K. Mansfield, said it was "worthless" and had "no probable certainty of hitting the object aimed at, and the recoil is too great to be fired with ease" (quoted in Gorenfeld 2008: 42). The horse pistol was a percussion cap, single-shot muzzleloader with a short effective range but serious stopping power. In 1845, Lieutenant (later Major General) James Carleton, 1st Dragoons, reported some of his men used this weapon to hunt buffalo in Nebraska.

The .44-caliber Colt Model 1848 Dragoon revolver began to replace the horse pistol in the late 1840s, but many cavalrymen kept the Model 1842 as a backup weapon or even their lone pistol throughout much of the 1850s. This is a First Model pistol, produced between 1848 and 1850. The six-round cylinder of this pistol greatly increased the cavalryman's firepower, giving him five or six shots instead of only one. Owing to the danger of accidentally discharging the pistol, a wise soldier left one chamber empty and only loaded it if he was sufficiently well informed to know a fight was imminent. Many individuals also carried an extra loaded cylinder that could be quickly snapped into place. Having multiple shots helped balance out the disparity between the cavalryman's rate of fire and that of an Apache armed with a bow. (NRA Museums, NRAmuseums.com)

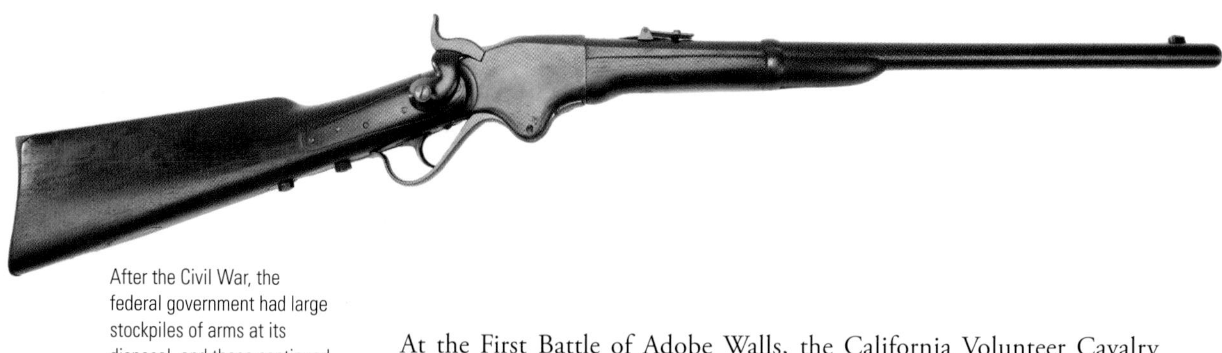

After the Civil War, the federal government had large stockpiles of arms at its disposal, and these continued to be issued for many years. There were two main cavalry carbines. The first was the .52-caliber Sharps breechloader, featuring a paper or linen cartridge and a percussion cap. A more potent weapon was the .56-56 Spencer carbine shown here. This was a lever-action, seven-shot repeater with a copper rimfire cartridge loaded through a tube in the butt. (NRA Museums, NRAmuseums.com)

At the First Battle of Adobe Walls, the California Volunteer Cavalry carried a Model 1859 Sharps carbine, a Model 1861 Colt Navy revolver, and a Model 1840 cavalry saber. In 1865, 5,000 .58-caliber Springfield Model 1861 rifled muskets were converted from muzzleloaders to breechloaders. Called the Springfield Model 1865 Breechloading Rifle (aka First Allin Conversion; aka Springfield "Trapdoor" Rifle), it used a rimfire cartridge. Issued to the infantry, many of these breechloaders found their way into the hands of the cavalry. The next year marked the debut of the Springfield Model 1866, or Second Allin Conversion, which modified the .58-caliber Springfield Model 1863 rifled musket to take a .50-70 centerfire cartridge. Both weapons had a 40in barrel that was too cumbersome for fighting on horseback. The .50-70 Model 1868, or Third Allin Conversion, featured a 32.6in barrel, plus a few other slight modifications and the same cartridge.

CONDUCT IN BATTLE

Apache

While Apache tactics focused on mobility, they would fortify if necessary, choosing a rocky hill or similarly rough ground and piling up rocks to make crude walls. The Spanish called these forts *refugios*, and they could be made very quickly. Settlers and the US Cavalry soon found how useful these could be and imitated their construction techniques.

The Apache preferred ambush and hit-and-run tactics, making full use of their intimate knowledge of the rough terrain. One of the main reasons for these tactics (besides living in an environment that favored them) was that Apache bands were quite small – rarely over a few dozen individuals – and so the loss of even one warrior had a significant effect on the group's ability to hunt and fight.

The Apache also had to contend with fighting against superior numbers. At the beginning of our period, war leaders could sometimes assemble a few

From 1874 the .45-70 Springfield Model 1873 "Trapdoor" rifle and carbine were issued. Based upon the .50-70 Springfield Model 1870 "Trapdoor" rifle but firing a .45-caliber copper centerfire cartridge, these became the weapons that would defeat the Apache. Both rifle and carbine underwent numerous modifications over the years, as did the cartridge. This example was produced sometime between 1879 and 1885. (NRA Museums, NRAmuseums.com)

hundred warriors; but attrition and division between those Apache who sought peace and those who continued to fight meant that in the 1870s and 1880s, war bands rarely exceeded 100 warriors, and were often only a few dozen in number. Guerrilla warfare was the only option. In many campaigns, the Apache were essentially engaged in one long, continuous fighting retreat, fighting to survive rather than to conquer.

"Soldiering in the Southwest – the rescue of Corporal Scott." This engraving by Frederic Remington appeared on the cover of the August 21, 1886 edition of *Harper's Weekly* and shows an incident in the Pinto Mountains of Mexico during the Geronimo campaign. Two of Corporal Edward Scott's comrades pick up the wounded soldier under heavy fire. Many men lost their lives this way, as the Apache would let a wounded and helpless man live, using him as bait for his comrades. The officer shown is Lieutenant Powhattan H. Clarke of the 10th Cavalry, who received the Medal of Honor for the deed. Scott, of Troop K, lived but lost part of his leg. In a letter to his mother dated May 10, 1886, Clarke wrote, "My dear Mother ... Our troop has been very highly complimented and the Captain is the hero of the hour. Do not tell me about the colored troops there is not a troop in the U.S. Army that I would trust my life to as quickly as this K troop of ours. I have seen them only once but it was in a place where a stampede would have meant massacre. The firing was at 200 yards from rocks nearly over our heads. No men could have been more determined and cooler than these same darkies were and as for their officers they like them and will risk themselves for them. The wounded Corporal has had to have his leg cut off, the ball that shattered it lodging in the other instep. This man rode seven miles without a groan, remarking to the Captin that he had seen forty men in one fight in a worse fix than he was. Such have I found the colored soldier." (LoC)

Once in a fight, the Apache tried to inflict as many losses as possible before disengaging. The high losses among cavalry officers and Apache scouts show that the Apache focused on eliminating these individuals. They knew that if an officer went down, the men were more likely to become disorganized and withdraw. Picking off the Apache scouts was of prime importance because these men were the cavalry's eyes, ears, and guides. There was also a strong personal motivation to kill those whom the Apache saw as traitors.

If the cavalry was in hot pursuit, the Apache tried to lure them into ambushes with a few warriors or women as bait, or they would leave a trail for the cavalry to follow. If the cavalry grew suspicious of these tricks, the Apache could set up a simple ambush without bait. The terrain was such that crossing the mountains on horseback meant there were few available routes, making it easy for the Apache to predict where the cavalry would go.

If the cavalry withdrew first, the Apache would pursue them only for as long as the terrain allowed them to do so in relative safety, while others in the band collected any equipment and mounts the cavalry left behind. The Apache also spied on the cavalry camp to learn the cavalry's routine and then raid the camp for horses. At Ojo Caliente on September 4, 1879, Victorio's band killed five soldiers guarding the herd of Company E, 9th Cavalry, and drove away the entire herd. The Apache warriors waited patiently over several days as the herd ate up the grass nearest the camp, until the herd had to be driven out of sight and earshot. One group of about a dozen warriors waited at the spot where the troopers were in the habit of resting and attacked them, while a second group drove off the horses and a third group sealed off the valley to grab any horses instinctively trying to get back to camp.

The Kiowa-Apache fought in the style of the larger Plains tribes. There was little natural cover and so these groups favored massed charges, attempting to close quickly. These charges were supported by men firing from the prone position using what cover they could. At Adobe Walls and other battles,

Cañon de L'or – soldiers repulsing an attack by Apache, 1870. While this is certainly a posed shot considering the bulkiness of the cameras of the day, it does demonstrate the rough terrain the soldiers had to fight in. If this had been a real fight, they would have hidden in the crevasses and become all but invisible. (LoC)

snipers hid in the tall grass to fire at the US soldiers. While this didn't afford them the bulletproof protection of the rocks in Arizona and New Mexico, it did hide them quite well.

US Cavalry

The tactics of the US Cavalry adapted slowly over the period. In the early days, tactics were quite basic, with the Dragoons advancing in close order or using simple movements such as the pincer attack used in the battle of Cieneguilla.

Upton's Tactics stressed that firing by file was the most important and common type of fire to be used, and that officers should train their men in this in preference to all other types of fire. Each man would fire in turn and in rapid succession, keeping up a continuous fire to intimidate the enemy and suppress their return fire, while their comrades had a chance to reload. When advancing in line of battle, the officer and sergeant were expected to advance slightly forward of the line to encourage them and maintain discipline of movement. Orders, especially while skirmishing over broken ground, would be given via the bugler.

Given the nature of the war, Upton's skirmishing instructions were the most important. The main firing line would have the men at five paces from each other, the distance varying depending on terrain and numbers. The manual suggested that there be a small company reserve about 150 paces behind the firing line to relieve the injured or fatigued, and to supply the fighting men with cartridges when they ran short. The manual stressed

This print from *Harper's Weekly*, titled "A new cavalry drill," dates to 1885 and shows the 6th Cavalry drilling in the region around Fort Bayard, New Mexico, and firing over their horses, which have been trained to lie flat on the ground. In many real engagements, the horses didn't have to be trained to lie still since they were often the first casualties. (LoC)

individual action during a skirmish, while each individual also had to keep in mind his part in the greater scheme of the skirmish. When an individual advanced, he should always do so firing.

Of course in an actual fight much of this planning went out the window. Given the Apaches' ability to strike without warning, the cavalry were usually reacting, not acting. Firing in file gave way to individual opportunity fire, and formations disintegrated as the men sought protection behind rocks in the broken terrain.

Cavalry tactics changed radically with the use of Apache scouts. Now the cavalry was able to take the war to the enemy and set up ambushes of their own. In one early battle in May 1870, Lieutenant Howard Cushing went after some Apache raiders with the help of an Apache guide who was able to follow their trail as they doubled back and went over rocks in an attempt to hide their passage. Once the raiders' camp was located, Cushing waited until dark and then quietly surrounded it. Then the group opened fire at the wickiups from all sides, trusting the rough ground to give them protection from friendly fire.

The cavalry often found that once they had closed with the enemy, their job had already been done for them. The scouts were usually ordered not to bring on a firefight and to wait until the main body arrived, but overeager Apache braves often attacked their hostile brethren and finished the fight before the cavalry arrived.

Cieneguilla

March 30, 1854

OPPOSITE A West Lipan Apache warrior, *c.*1857. The Lipan lived in western Texas. Like their cousins in New Mexico and Arizona, they moved in small bands with no central command. This caused problems with the Mexicans, Texans, and Americans because while one band might make peace, others would not feel constrained by this decision. Buffalo hunting was the mainstay of their traditional survival strategy and they quickly adopted horses in the Spanish period, becoming expert riders. Thus culturally they were a middle ground between the Apache of the Desert Southwest and the Kiowa-Apache of the Plains. (Photo by Hulton Archive/Getty Images)

BACKGROUND TO BATTLE

The conflict that led to the battle of Cieneguilla started because of numerous complaints of Apache raids on settlers. On March 5, 1854, a company of the 2nd Dragoons from Fort Union got into a fight with a band of Jicarilla in which two Dragoons were killed and four wounded. The Apache lost five men, including Chief Lobo. During their retreat, the Apache made off with 200 head of Fort Union's cattle and killed two herdsmen. The Jicarilla, indeed all native tribes, were feeling the pressure of increased settlement on their traditional lands. Hunting was becoming poor and areas that had once been used for agriculture and gathering had become rangeland. The Jicarilla were a small group, only a few hundred individuals in several bands with no central leadership. Their way of life was threatened and so warriors increasingly turned to raiding in order to feed their families.

In late March, a large group of Jicarilla passed through the area and the Government forces suspected they were the culprits. First Lieutenant John Wynn Davidson was ordered to "watch and control their movements" (Johnson *et al.* 2009: 27), but not bring on an engagement. He led 60 men of Company I and a detachment of Company F, 1st Dragoons, into the Embudo Mountains a few miles away from the Rio Grande. The Dragoons were armed with the .69-caliber Springfield Model 1847 musketoon and the .54-caliber Springfield Model 1842 "horse pistol." Some also carried the

.44-caliber Colt Dragoon revolver. Private Peter Weldon of Company F recalled that the troops went in with 40 rounds of musketoon ammunition, 20 pistol cartridges, and 30 revolver rounds for those who had revolvers.

Early on the morning of March 30, the Dragoons left the village of Cieneguilla, following the trail to the Embudo Mountains. In front went two soldiers and a scout, Jesus Silva. Davidson and the remainder of the command followed them for a time but soon veered off onto another trail that headed for the mountains. Why Davidson sent his scout off in another direction is unclear. Soon the main body came upon fresh tracks of numerous Apache and followed them into a narrow defile below the ridge on which the Jicarilla were camped. They proceeded up the bottom of the canyon along the Apache trail until they reached a rock outcrop and increasing slopes that impeded further progress. Then they climbed the bank to their right to a gently sloping area near the base of the ridge just above the canyon bottom, and dismounted about 375yd from the creek.

Just as the Dragoons were coming into the canyon or heading up the slope, the Apache shouted a challenge to them. The band had heard the noise

Shee-zah-nan-tan, a Jicarilla Apache brave in characteristic costume, northern New Mexico, 1874. Finely dressed in a fringed buckskin shirt and pants, this man shows the trappings of wealth. His hair is braided, while on the march the hair was generally left loose. A riding crop hangs from his wrist. (LoC)

A Jicarilla Apache brave and his wife, lately wedded, 1874. This photo affords a good look at a quiver, generally made from the hide of a coyote or mountain lion. "We often made quivers for our arrows from the skin of the mountain lion. These were very pretty and very durable" (Geronimo 1971: 65). The bow is carried in a hide case to protect it from the elements. The bracelets on the woman and ring on the man are most likely copper or silver. Gold was considered forbidden, it being sacred to their god Ussen. The Apache figured that since gold had no practical use, it was for their god, and believed that when the settlers dug in the earth to extract it their actions made Ussen angry and brought about earthquakes. (LoC)

of the approaching horses echoing up the narrow canyon and had already sent their elderly, women, and children safely away into the forested gullies south of camp. The warriors were now ready to fight and probably had time to discuss strategy. Davidson decided to attack, feeling a challenge should not go unanswered.

The Dragoons tied their horses to trees and Davidson ordered eight men under the command of Assistant Surgeon D.L. Magruder to guard them. The remainder divided into two platoons, with the first platoon led by First Sergeant William C. Holbrook advancing on the right and the second under Sergeant William Kent on the left. They struggled up the steep, 90ft slope, which made the smooth leather soles of their footwear slip from beneath them. Firing commenced when they got about 100–160yd from the camp. The Dragoons ascended in tight bunches and made easy targets for the Apache hiding behind trees and rocks above them. One platoon ascended via a narrow draw a short way to the north, while the other headed straight up the slope from where the horses had been tied.

The following description of the battle has been compiled from an examination of all accounts from both sides and a thorough archaeological survey of the battlefield.

Jicarilla Apache and the 1st Dragoons at Cieneguilla, March 30, 1854

MAP KEY

1 0800hrs: The Dragoons approach up the valley and are challenged by the Apache on the ridge with a war whoop.

2 *c*.0803hrs: First Lieutenant John Wynn Davidson orders his men to tether their horses in a valley below the Apache camp. He leaves eight men under Assistant Surgeon D.L. Magruder to guard them.

3 *c*.0805hrs: Two companies – First Sergeant William C. Holbrook's to the north and Sergeant William Kent's to the south – charge up the side of the ridge to attack the camp.

4 *c*.0810hrs: The Apache retreat from the camp; but the retreat is a ruse and they circle around.

5 *c*.0815–0915hrs: The Apache hit the horseholders in the valley, attacking from all sides. The horseholders call for help and the main force returns. The dismounted Dragoons fight off several attacks for at least an hour; some reports say two hours.

6 *c*.0915–0925hrs: With losses rising, Davidson calls for a withdrawal across the creek and up the steep slopes of the ridge beyond to the northeast.

7 *c*.0925–0935hrs: The Dragoons reach the top of the ridge after a brief break only to find the Apache warriors already there. They fight for about ten minutes before the Dragoons withdraw along the ridge.

8 *c*.0935–1030hrs: The Dragoons have to stop their retreat several times to fight off Apache attacks.

9 *c*.1030hrs: After one final attack by the Apache, Davidson orders a withdrawal off the ridge and down into the adjacent canyon.

10 *c*.1030–dusk: After the Dragoons enter the canyon, the Apache stop attacking. The Dragoons follow the canyon for several miles before stopping to rest. After reaching the main road to Taos from Cieneguilla, they head back to Cantonment Burgwin.

Battlefield environment

The area of the battle of Cieneguilla was forested mountainside cut by steep valleys topped with narrow ridges. The soil was damp and slick, hampering the movement of the Dragoons in their smooth leather footwear. The Apache moccasin was much better adapted for moving quickly and silently over such terrain because the soft-soled buckskin gripped better. The sides of the ridges had numerous trees and large rocks, making for good cover. In places the underbrush was thick. While anyone firing a gun would give away their position with the puff of black powder, an Apache using a bow would have been hard to spot. The Apache had two more advantages: they were rested, while the Dragoons had to ride to the battle; and they had been camping there for several days and thus knew the terrain intimately. There was the added psychological advantage of being in home territory while the Dragoons were marching into an area that was poorly known to them, and their guide, Jesus Silva, was off on another trail and not with them for the final advance, battle, or retreat. The Apache warriors could hope for reinforcements from the nearby Picuris village, while the Dragoons had no help closer than a day away.

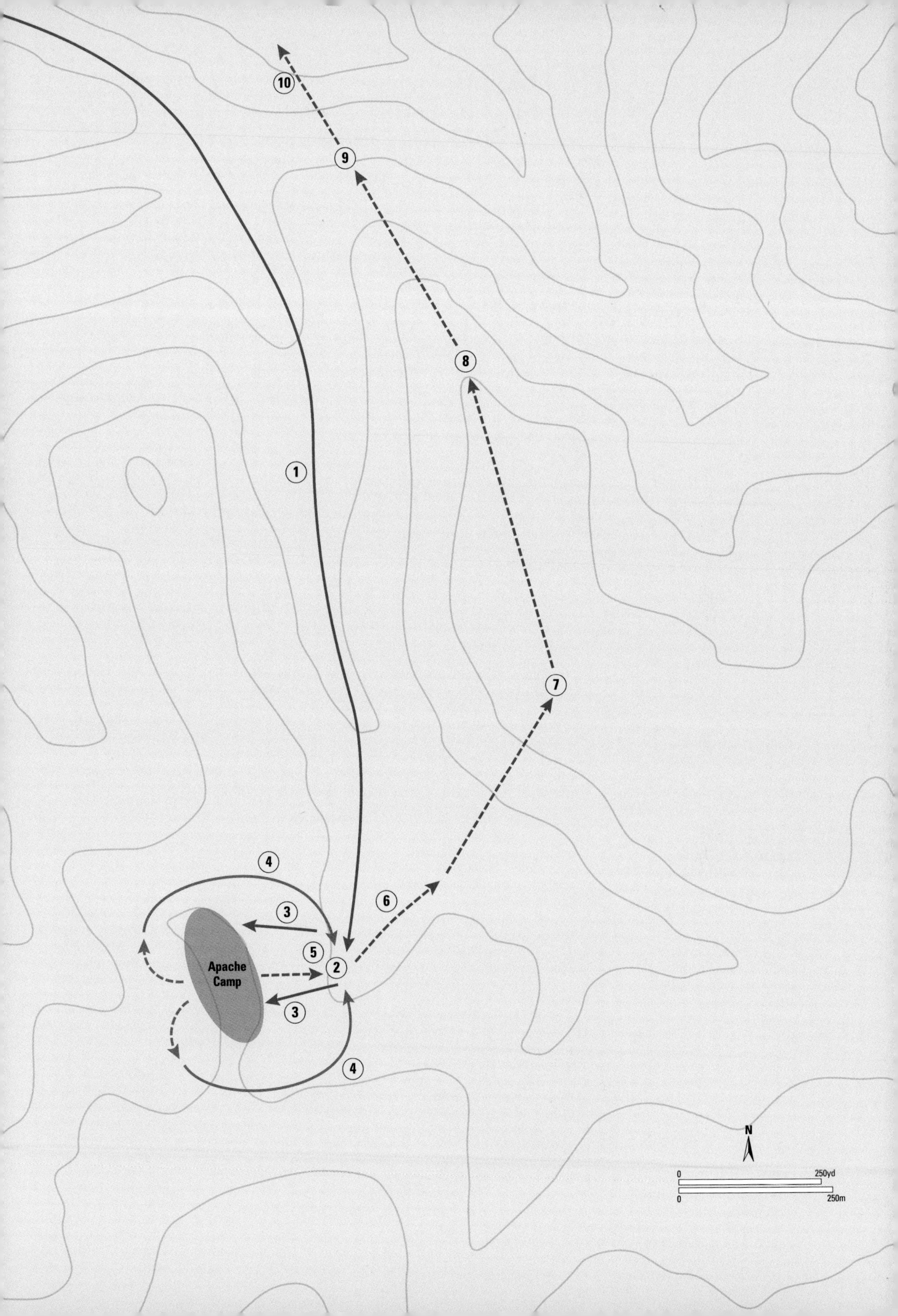

10
9
8
1
7
4
6
3
5
2
Apache Camp
3
4
N
0
250yd
0
250m

INTO COMBAT

Once up the slope, the two Dragoon detachments each formed a line and attacked the camp from two different directions, catching the defenders in crossfire. The camp was located on the narrow ridge top about 175yd from the dismount point. They took the camp within a few minutes, with the Apache retreating shortly after the Dragoons entered. Sergeant Kent was killed upon entering the camp and four more soldiers were killed either on the slope or in the camp. An unknown number were wounded.

The retreat was a ruse. The Apache went around the ridge and attacked the troops guarding the horses, shooting from behind trees and launching arrows down from up the slope, safe from the short-ranged musketoons. The horseholders, greatly outnumbered, shouted for help, and the main body of soldiers hurried back, leaving their dead behind. The Apache had played a favorite trick – they drew away the main body of troops while coming around behind to take the animals and supplies. The Apache attacked from several directions at once, and it is a credit to the steadiness of Magruder and the others that the Dragoons weren't wiped out.

While the reinforcements were able to drive the Apache back, the Dragoons were surrounded and pinned down for one or two hours. The Apache fired from high ground and from behind cover. Now it was the Dragoons who were caught in crossfire; but unlike the Apache, they had nowhere to run. More soldiers fell, much of their ammunition was depleted, and the men started showing signs of crumbling morale and exhaustion. There were few large rocks to hide behind at the bottom of the canyon, while the Apache on higher ground had many to use as shelter.

Private James Strowbridge of Company I recalled they were only up in the camp four or five minutes before the attack on the horses commenced. Once they returned,

> The Indians in a moment, or two, made a charge on us from three sides at once. We repulsed them again & were then ordered to screen ourselves behind any trees or breastwork that we could get. We surrounded the horses in a sort of circle, and

Mechanics' corral, Fort Union, New Mexico. Those who stayed in the fort were just as important as those who went on the march. Maintaining equipment was a never-ending job thanks to the rough roads and trails that quickly wore out wagons, artillery limbers, horseshoes, tack, and uniforms. During the Civil War, this fort would help protect settlers from attacks by the Apache and other tribes, as well as incursions from Confederate Texas. Conditions remained primitive in frontier forts until the 1880s, after which they slowly began to improve. (Fort Union National Monument)

while in that position the Indians made two more charges on us from three sides at once. We drove them back each time.

There was some times 20 minutes, some times half an hour, elapsed between these charges. Afterwards they would charge together from, some times one side, & some times another. The men from one side, would go to the other where the Indians were charging to assist in repelling them. We repulsed them every time. We fought at that place from an hour and a half, to two hours, we lost some men there and killed some Indians. I saw two Indians fall myself. (Quoted in Johnson *et al.* 2009: 157)

Bezaleel W. Armstrong graduated from the US Military Academy and was made brevet second lieutenant, 1st Dragoons, in 1845. He became a second lieutenant of the 2nd Dragoons the following year and served in the Mexican–American War at Vera Cruz and Mexico City in 1847–48. He died in 1849 at the age of 26. This daguerreotype was taken *c.*1846. West Point graduates left the school with four years of training in conventional warfare and were usually immediately assigned to the West. The class of 1872 saw 96 percent of the graduates sent there. They had received no instruction from officers who had fought the Apache or any other tribes, and thus guerrilla warfare was new to them. They were also ill-prepared physically and mentally for the rigors of the Desert Southwest. Memoirs and diaries frequently reflect the officers' shock at their transfer from the spit and polish of West Point to some dreary frontier fort. A large percentage of men immediately fell sick and had to be taken off duty for a time before that duty had properly begun. Once at their post and in a state to serve, a wise officer listened to veterans in order to bring himself up to speed. After the Civil War there was an influx of veteran officers who, while generally only having experience in pitched battles, were at least seasoned under fire. Officers generally stayed with their units for several years, getting to know the men and the terrain. This greatly helped with unit cohesion and effectiveness, although of course being the Army, an order could come at any time whisking a favorite officer away to another post. (Photo by Time Life Pictures/US Army/National Archives/The LIFE Picture Collection/Getty Images)

Davidson ordered a retreat to a nearby small hill about 175yd away. Once there, they were attacked on all sides. Davidson realized the position was a poor one and switched direction to cross the creek and ascend the steep slopes of a ridge a half-mile to the northeast. During these movements they led what horses still survived, essentially disarming anyone leading a horse. The Dragoons halted halfway up the slope to rest. Strowbridge recalled:

We rested there a minute or two and saw the Indians crossing the ravine to get on top of the mountain to head us off. We moved up on the hill further as it looked still better as a fighting position, I suppose that is the reason we moved there. We got on top of the hill and faced the Indians & remained in that position some fifteen minutes. The Indians kept surrounding us & were in our front & on both sides. (Quoted in Johnson *et al.* 2009: 157)

The Dragoons found the Apache waiting for them at the top. There followed a brisk ten-minute firefight before Davidson led his men along the ridge. During this movement they were attacked several times. At last Davidson, who had shown great fighting spirit even after being stuck by an arrow, ordered his men to leave the dead, gather the wounded, and retreat down the ridge to the adjacent canyon. They had lost 17 more men during the retreat, with half the survivors wounded. Private James A. Bronson said:

The moment we reached the summit of the mountain [ridge], they attacked us, there, there was an engagement of ten minutes. The command after this engagement changed its direction to the left, we were then moving on the ridge of a mountain. We had moved but 20 or 30 rods from when we had our first

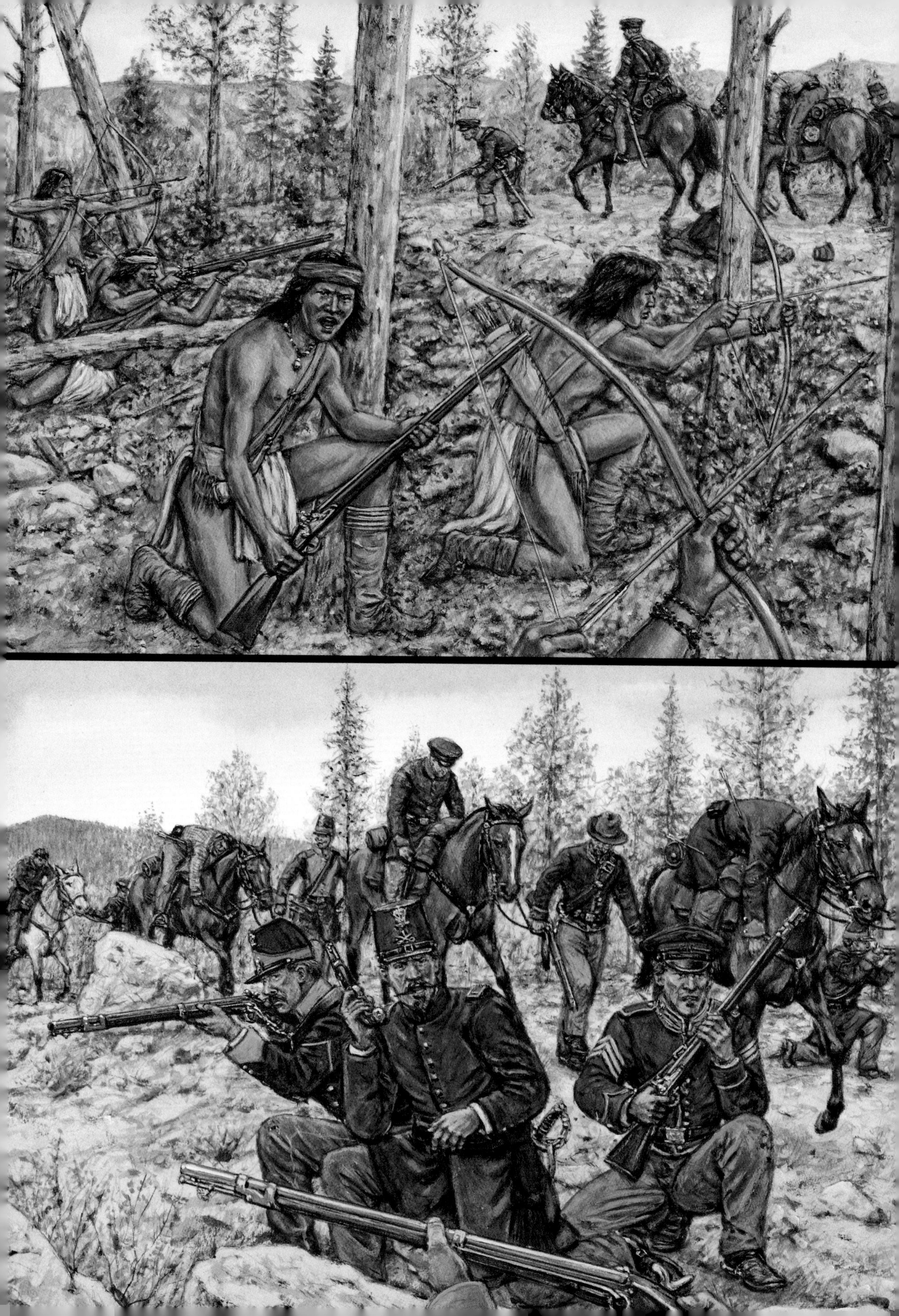

A desperate chase

Apache view: At this point in the battle the Apache have been harrying the Dragoons for at least two hours and inflicting serious casualties. Angered by the unprovoked attack on their village, they are closing in for the kill. The Dragoons are showing fight and the Apache remain cautious, using whatever cover they can. Archaeological evidence shows that at this point in the battle, the Apache used more bows than guns, perhaps because they were running low on ammunition, or perhaps they wanted to take advantage of the higher rate of fire the bow offered. The bow also had a better effective range than anything the Dragoons carried, although this would have been reduced by the vegetation. The weary column of retreating Dragoons made a good target as warriors popped out from behind trees to fire at them.

US view: The Dragoons, after initially thinking they would carry the day when they easily pushed the Apache out of their ridge-top village, found themselves victims of a double envelopment and had to hurry back to save their horseholders. The entire force was surrounded and fought for more than an hour before returning to the ridge and beating a hasty retreat. By this time, most men are dead or wounded and they have lost most of their horses. As Private James A. Bronson of Company B remembered, "The wounded men were then placed with the horses & the others defended the flanks & rear. We moved slowly on in that manner for nearly half a mile, being attacked several times by the Indians, in going that distance but they were repelled each time by the soldiers" (quoted in Johnson *et al.* 2009: 150). The archaeology tells a different story, one of panic. The archaeologists recovered large amounts of dropped gear, ammunition, and unused percussion caps.

> engagement, on top of the mountain, when the Indians attacked us in rear.
>
> The wounded men were then placed with the horses & the others defended the flanks & rear. We moved slowly on in that manner for nearly half a mile, being attacked several times by the Indians, in going that distance but they were repelled each time by the soldiers. (Quoted in Johnson *et al.* 2009: 151)

The archaeologists found numerous clusters of artifacts along the ridge such as percussion caps and arrowheads, marking where the soldiers stopped to make a stand. As the Dragoons neared the saddle where the trail to Cieneguilla was located, they found the side slope was less steep here, and so the soldiers made a final stumbling retreat down the side of the ridge to the adjacent canyon. Private Peter Weldon of Company F recalled that he felt he "could stand up no longer" (quoted in Gorenfeld 2008: 43), while Private James A. Bronson of Company B recalled:

> At the end of that distance we came to where the mountain led to a deep ravine or canon, when & where the Indians appeared to make their great charge, & closed in up on us. This charge was also repelled. Capt. Davidson was also wounded at this time, and also several men who were standing close beside me. Capt. Davidson then spoke so as to be heard by all around & said, "don't get excited, men. Keep Cool. I have often been in worse places than this."
>
> The shower of arrows at this point had been so great, that the ground had become completely strewn with them. The fighting men at this time, were but few in number, as the majority of them had been wounded, before reaching this point, and I heard those defending the rear & flanks complaining that they were completely wearred [*sic*] out. Capt. Davidson then called for his horse, which the bugler was leading. It was brought to him and he ordered the command to mount

The Model 1847 musketoon is shown here along with the 1847-pattern Grimsley saddle. The Grimsley saddle was adopted for the US Cavalry in 1847 and was used until replaced by the McClellan saddle in 1859. Many officers continued to use it after this time because they had become accustomed to it, and a well-cared-for saddle that has been broken in is far more comfortable than a brand-new one issued by the quartermaster. Designed by Thornton Grimsley of St. Louis, it was a major improvement over the Ringgold saddle, which during the Mexican–American War was the subject of many complaints. The Grimsley saddle was more comfortable due to its deer-hair stuffing under the quilted seat. It was the first US Cavalry saddle that was encased in wet rawhide, strengthening it and making it lighter than the Ringgold, which used heavy bands of iron for reinforcement. (National Archives)

and move on. Then commenced, what I considered, a retreat from the Indians, and an eye witness, must have acknowledged that we were beaten by over numbers & hard fighting …

> As we reached the foot of the hill, which was some forty yards in height, I turned in the saddle and saw on the brow of the hill which we had left, a large body of Indians, there must have been sixty or seventy, and also others on the two flanks, who were making the best use of their arms that they could against us. After following the ravine some hundred yards, or near that distance, I saw two Indians, by themselves, to the right of the ravine, one of them fired his piece and struck the croup of the horse in front of me, this was the last of the Indians that I saw. (Quoted in Johnson *et al.* 2009: 152)

Strowbridge had a vivid recollection of the retreat:

> The last time we faced about was just before we went down on the other side of the hill. We kept our position there for near twenty minutes, I think, fighting the Indians, intending to hold the position. I was sitting behind a tree trying to get a shot at an Indian, a shot struck the ground by my side, and another passed between Private Newhand's legs as he was squatting down, he said it wasn't best for us to stay there as we were not sheltered. The Indians at this time commenced firing arrows very fast, you could see fifteen or twenty falling on the ground at once. As we raised up to change our position I heard some body say that the Lieutenant was wounded. I turned around and saw an arrow sticking in his shoulder, he said never mind it is nothing. Corporal Dempsey, I think, pulled the arrow out, the Capt. was wounded himself through the leg by a ball, & one of his thumbs was shot in two.
>
> About this time Sergt. Holbrook came walking along by me, and asked me if I could get him a horse, he said I am shot and can not go any further on foot. I got him a horse and he tried to mount, but he was so weak he couldn't. He was very bloody, he had two arrows sticking in him, one in his back nearly to the feathers. When he tried to mount the horse, he fell over backwards & died. I can not tell how long afterwards we stayed at this place. This was the last fight that we made. Capt. Davidson gave the command then to mount and forward and we moved down the hill. There were but few left who were not wounded. We put the wounded men on the horses, a wounded man on a horse, and a well man behind him, we retreated in that manner from the field. (Quoted in Johnson *et al.* 2009: 158)

OPPOSITE This work by Edward Vebell (1921–) depicts a US Dragoon, *c.*1848. He carries a .69-caliber Springfield Model 1847 musketoon and a Model 1840 cavalry saber that had a 36in blade. He would have also carried a .54-caliber Springfield Model 1842 "horse pistol," although this is not shown. The yellow worsted headband of his cap shows him to be of the 2nd Dragoons. The cap had a flap that could be let down to shield the neck from the elements. Note the white buff saber belt with cross-strap arrangement to hold both the saber on the left side and the musketoon on the right. Like many men on the frontier, he has added a few personally purchased items to round out his kit, in this case some fringed leather boot covers, no doubt to make shining them after a long desert ride much easier. (Illustration by Ed Vebell/Getty Images)

At this point the Apache stopped attacking. The Dragoons had been driven off and much booty captured. There was no sense in risking more casualties for no real purpose. The Dragoons followed the canyon for several miles before stopping for a rest. Then they moved to the Taos–Cieneguilla road and headed back toward Cantonment Burgwin.

The Jicarilla Apache had won one of their greatest victories over the US Army. The Apache had about 100–130 warriors, probably led by Chief Flechas Rayada, who had succeeded Chief Lobo after he was killed in a skirmish with Dragoons from Fort Union a few weeks before. In the battle, 22 Dragoons were killed and 23 wounded, at least one mortally, making it the cavalry's worst defeat in the West at that time. In addition, 45 Army horses – almost all the detachment's mounts – were killed or lost. Apache casualties are unclear, US Army estimates ranging from two to 50. Apache estimates are vague, but Chief Chacon mentioned specifically that Chief Pacheco died there.

This bloody episode led to a court of inquiry into Davidson's handling of the fight, but he was eventually exonerated. In his official report, Davidson stated:

> After a desperate fight of near three hours I was compelled to withdraw with my wounded whom I succeeded in bringing to Taos.
>
> The melancholy duty now revolves on me of reporting twenty two of my gallant command killed upon the field, and twenty three wounded, and upwards of forty five horses killed and lost in action. I refer to the accompanying list of killed and wounded for details. There were from my own observation and that of the Pueblo Indians who went out with Major [George A.H.] Blake to bring in the dead, upwards of three hundred Apache and Utah warriors who opposed me. (Quoted in Johnson *et al.* 2009: 103)

Davis claimed that 30–40 Apache were killed, and mentioned the Ute (Utah) tribe being involved in the fight, but later investigation shows this was doubtful and that his report was exaggerated in numerous particulars in his favor. The day after the battle a force was sent out to retrieve the soldiers' bodies. Lieutenant David Bell reported on the carnage:

> I have conversed with Major Blake, Maj. [Philip H.] Thompson and Mr. [James H.] Quinn all of whom visited Cieneguilla the next day and the result of their stories is this that 5 men only were found dead upon the side of the hill up which Davidson advanced, and it is by no means certain that they were dead when the retreat was ordered, while 14 men were found on the hill side down which the flight took place, and two or three more in the ravine below. This cannot be denied and it proves that a command of 57 Dragoons retreated without an attempt to preserve order when they had lost 5 of their number.
>
> Davidson says in his official

> report, which I have read, that there were 250 or 300 Apache and Utah warriors in the fight that he fought for three hours and has every reason to believe he killed a large number of Indians. In the first place there were no Utahs in the fight & secondly there were not more than 130 warriors (Apaches) in it, as [Kit] Carson or any person who followed them will tell you. If 50 or 60 of these had been killed the rest must have been wounded if any sort of usual proportion between killed and wounded obtained.
>
> As to fighting three hours that is the most ridiculously absurd assertion in the whole report. A Cartridge Box (cavalry) holds some 30 to 50 Cartridges. How long would it take a man to fire this number of Cartridges assuming that he fired all of them? But in the excitement of action most men will lose a large portion of their ammunition. I think any reasonable man will agree that Davidson's fight never lasted 30 minutes, his assertion to the contrary notwithstanding.
>
> In regard to the probable number killed I forgot to say that it is a remarkable fact that the number of lodges after the fight was the same as before and we were informed in every Mexican settlement through which we passed in the pursuit, that the Indians said they had lost only two men in the battle. (Quoted in Johnson *et al.* 2009: 27)

Bell's complaints prompted an investigation into the battle. Bell was correct about the Apache numbers. The Indian Agent for the area, Christopher "Kit" Carson, who had met with the Jicarilla chiefs a few weeks before, reported the Jicarilla numbered about 100 warriors and their families. They claimed they hadn't done any raiding and hadn't fought the cavalry from Fort Union. Although not present at the battle, Chief Chacon, the leading chief of this band of Jicarilla, stated, "At the time the fight began, the Indians were making clay pottery and that some of the Indians were even on their knees begging for peace. The Americans killed a chief Pacheco, and a ball cut out the entrails of a woman, who survived. About 50 Indians were killed at Cieneguilla" (quoted in Johnson *et al.* 2009: 20). There is also this Apache account from 1909:

> The Jicarilla moved their camp to a mountain east of Picuris. When they had been there four days the Americans came again on horseback early in the morning. They halted and one approached to pass the Apache a paper. An Apache took it from the hands of the officer and tore it up. Someone shot the person who had handed the paper, wounding him in the arm. Then the soldiers opened the fight. They had halted on the plain with their horses and were shooting in different directions, the Indians having surrounded them. The Apache kept on shooting and killing the soldiers until only two were left. Four of the Apache were killed. They took all the arms of the soldiers and the money from their clothes, a large sum. From there the Apache moved to the west side of the Rio Grande. (Quoted in Johnson *et al.* 2009: 21)

A nearby tribe called the Picuris was allied with the Jicarilla and according to oral tradition written down in 1965, the Jicarilla asked for their assistance, but it arrived after the battle: "As soon as the fight had started, the Apaches sent a man to our pueblo for help. A band of our warriors left to go help the Apaches, but by the time they got there, the battle was over and they saw all

"Jicarilla fiesta." Jicarilla Apache, most on horseback, moving toward an encampment. Living on a reservation in Oklahoma, these Jicarilla have taken on some aspects of Plains Indian culture, especially the tepee. Photo by Edward Curtis, *c.*1905. (LoC)

the dead soldiers on the ground full of arrows" (quoted in Johnson *et al.* 2009: 22).

Mr. Head, special agent to the Indians, reported that Chief Flechas Rayada commanded the Apache in battle, there were 150 warriors, and they suffered only three killed. The chief sent a message via Mr. Head that he would fight again if he could draw the Dragoons into bad terrain, but was willing to give up the captured arms and horses if peace could be made. It was not to be. The defeat at Cieneguilla was the main event that led to a concerted campaign against the Jicarilla – a campaign the United States eventually won. The Jicarilla were relocated to a reservation they still inhabit today.

The archaeological survey also contradicts Davidson's report. A cluster of artifacts such as percussion caps and soldiers' buttons show that the fight where the horses were tied was indeed on low ground; numerous percussion caps were found here and 60 percent had been fired, showing the men kept their nerve even though they were surrounded. In the later fight on the ridge, only 30 percent had been fired, indicating the Dragoons' increasing fatigue and panic.

The survey revealed that the retreat was not as orderly as Davidson claimed: the route was littered with dropped ammunition, unused percussion caps, and other debris. It appears the Dragoons were nearing panic at this point. Finally, Davidson reported that there were more than 300 warriors, but the camp was too small for so many; and while they outnumbered the Dragoons, they had to fight with inferior weapons. Their use of terrain and deception, and Davidson's own overconfidence, decided the outcome of the battle.

First Adobe Walls

November 25, 1864

BACKGROUND TO BATTLE

Satanta, sitting for a portrait sometime between 1870 and 1875. (LoC)

The Civil War drained the frontier of troops, and many tribes took the opportunity to raid settlements and try to regain some of their territory. Various tribes in the Indian Territory sided with the South, while a minority sided with the North. On the southern Great Plains, the Kiowa-Apache rose up, encouraged by Confederate Brigadier General Albert Pike, who commanded the Department of the Indian Territory. Federal officials tried to get the Kiowa-Apache on the plains onto their side by encouraging them to raid in Texas. It appears the Kiowa-Apache and their allies, the powerful Comanche, had little regard for either North or South and raided both sides, thrusting into Texas as well as hitting federal wagon trains.

On October 13, 1864, several hundred Comanche and Kiowa-Apache raided Young County, Texas. The terrified civilians retreated to a fortified home and held off the Indians for six hours. As usual, the Apache were loath to attack

Satanta

A Kiowa-Apache chief, Satanta (*c.*1820–78) was the son of Chief Red Tipi and a Spanish captive, and was the last war chief of his people. As a youth he fought the Cheyenne and Ute and raided all the way to Mexico. In 1864 he fought at the First Battle of Adobe Walls, where he tricked the cavalry force with fake bugle calls. He later tried the same trick when coming home to his settlement, blowing the order to charge to announce his arrival. To his delight, all his fellow Kiowa-Apache fled to the hills.

Satanta, Dohasan, and other chiefs signed the Treaty of the Little Arkansas River in 1865, but this didn't stop settlers from continuing to take their lands and so the warriors started raiding again. After Dohasan's death in 1866, the Kiowa-Apache descended into infighting, with Satanta leading one of the factions. He also raided white settlements and attacked wagon trains. He signed another peace treaty, the Medicine Lodge Treaty, in 1867, but once again white incursions and hotheaded warriors kept it from working. Major General Philip Sheridan's winter campaign of 1868–69 inflicted serious losses on the Kiowa-Apache and forced Satanta to surrender.

He was imprisoned for a short period, then released. By 1871, anger over a shortage of rations on the reservation led to more raids, culminating in the Salt Creek Massacre, in which seven teamsters were killed. Satanta and his men returned to the reservation and the chief was soon arrested. He remained in prison until 1873, when he was released on the promise of keeping his people in check. This didn't happen, and after a year of raids Satanta was arrested again. Facing a life sentence without hope of parole, he killed himself in 1878 by jumping headfirst out a window.

fortified positions. Instead, they kept the defenders inside with covering fire while their companions plundered the surrounding homes and herds. By the time help arrived the next day, the Indians had retreated, leaving behind 11 dead settlers, and carrying with them seven women and children as captives. They also took more than 1,000 head of cattle.

The Comanche and Kiowa-Apache moved to a scattering of winter camps along the Canadian River in Northern Texas, near the ruins of Adobe Walls, a fortified trading post established in 1845 and blown up and abandoned three years later. Soon some of the younger men went out to raid into Colorado and New Mexico, leaving behind a sizable force of warriors to defend the camps.

Kit Carson

A Wild West legend, Christopher "Kit" Carson (1809–68) was raised in Missouri and joined a wagon train headed west on the Santa Fe Trail in 1826. He became famous for his reliability, honesty, and knowledge of the land. Throughout the 1840s he acted as a guide for John Fremont on his many expeditions to the Pacific, which helped map the best routes for westward expansion. It also brought Carson into the national limelight and soon popular novels were being written about his exploits, both real and fictitious.

Carson got his first taste of large-scale battle in the Mexican–American War, where he distinguished himself. As a part of Brigadier General Stephen Kearny's army, he got into a tight spot on December 6, 1846, when the column was surrounded by Mexicans at San Pasqual, about 30 miles north of San Diego. For three days the Americans fought off the Mexicans; but the situation was becoming increasingly desperate, so Carson and two others snuck through enemy lines and ran all the way to San Diego, where they got reinforcements and saved Kearny's men.

After the war, Carson took up ranching in New Mexico. In 1854 he was appointed Indian Agent over the Apache and Ute, in which capacity he testified about the battle of Cieneguilla. At the onset of the Civil War, he organized volunteers for the Union in New Mexico Territory and fought at the Battle of Valverde in 1862. The following year he quelled the Navajo revolt, and in 1864 led a column against the Comanche and Kiowa-Apache at Adobe Walls. In 1865 he was commissioned a brigadier general, but his adventurous life had taken a toll on his health and he did not live much longer.

Christopher "Kit" Carson, famed Indian fighter and commander of the government forces at the battle of Adobe Walls. (LoC)

At this point they came to the attention of the Union-held forts in New Mexico, under the command of Major General James Carleton of the Department of New Mexico, who arrived at the settlements along the Rio Grande in September 1862 and instructed his troops on how to deal with hostile tribes: "The men are to be slain whenever and wherever they can be found. The women and children may be taken prisoners, but, of course, they are not to be killed" (quoted in Dunlay 2000: 492). To deal with the current crisis, he sent Colonel Kit Carson, an experienced Indian fighter. Carson set out from Fort Bascom on November 6 with two-and-a-half companies of the 1st California Cavalry, two companies of the 1st New Mexico Cavalry, a company of California infantry, and an artillery battery of two 12-pounder mountain howitzers commanded by Lieutenant George Pettis. All had been stationed in the Territory of New Mexico to protect it after ejecting a brief Confederate thrust into the region from Texas. Carson also had 75 Ute and Jicarilla Apache scouts, a surgeon, and a quartermaster. In total, he had 14 officers, 321 enlisted men, and 75 scouts. The presence of Jicarilla Apache going out to fight the Kiowa-Apache should come as no surprise. While they shared a language and many cultural traits, the Plains and Mountain Apache were hostile to one another. The Kiowa-Apache had made numerous raids on the Jicarilla, the Ute, and other tribes in New Mexico. The Jicarilla often referred to them as "bad neighbors."

Carson was supposed to neutralize the Indian threat by attacking them in their winter camps. His intention was not only to inflict casualties, but to destroy as much property as possible, punishing the tribes for their raids and making it harder for them to survive the winter. The column would be thrusting into the Texas Panhandle, the heartland of the Comanche and Kiowa-Apache. It was a daring move designed to strike a blow to their confidence and hit the problem at its source.

Carleton had written to Major General James Blunt, commanding in western Kansas, to coordinate with Carson by pushing west and trapping the Indians between the two columns. This converging-column strategy had worked well in the past and remained a favorite of the US Cavalry throughout the Indian Wars. The plan went awry when Confederate Major General Sterling Price invaded Missouri from Arkansas and headed west through the state toward Kansas. Blunt had to hurry to meet this new and more serious threat.

Comancheros (traders with the Indians) had reported the general location of the camps to the Army as being some 250 miles from Fort Bascom. Carson decided to set out with a single column that could be easily divided. His cavalry were supplied by pack mules, while the infantry would guard the wagon train, consisting of 27 wagons and an ambulance.

Apache scouts at Apache Lake, Sierra Blanca Range, 1873. The figure on the left appears to be holding arrows. While every Apache wanted to own a rifle, it was common practice to carry a bow as well. It could be used for hunting without announcing the hunter's location and saved on ammunition, which was always scarce. Even the Apache scouts had to justify every shot they used to their officers. Carson found Indian scouts who not only understood the enemy well, but had a burning desire for revenge. He had been their Indian Agent for a time so was able to pick reliable individuals whom he knew personally. He sent these scouts roving out along the front and flanks during the march. Commanding the artillery, Lieutenant George Pettis of Company K, 1st California Infantry was less enthusiastic about the scouts. In a memoir about the battle, he wrote: "The Indians with our command, on every night after making camp, being now on the war path, indulged in their war dance, which, although new to most of us, became almost intolerable, it being kept up each night until nearly daybreak, and until we became accustomed to their groans and howlings incident to the dance, it was impossible to sleep" (Pettis 1878: 11). (LoC)

Thus the faster and slower parts of the force could separate and each would still be supplied. Carson made sure the horses were all well shod before setting out on the long winter march.

The column headed out onto the vast, almost featureless plains, being stopped twice by snowstorms. Carson marched them in easy stages – he needed every man and mount fresh for a fight with an entirely mounted foe. On November 24 they camped about 30 miles from Adobe Walls. At around sunset, two of the Indian scouts returned and reported to Carson that they had located the Kiowa-Apache camp close to the old trading post, which acted as a prominent landmark in the vast grassland.

While relating the return of the scouts, Pettis makes an interesting remark about how the Indians were much more accustomed to picking out details in this seemingly featureless landscape. While the men were at rest in camp, the scouts suddenly leapt up and stared at a certain point to the east. None of the soldiers could see anything over there.

> Although the returning scouts were at least two miles distant, and, mounted on their ponies, were hardly discernible, yet the quick, sharp eye of our Indians made them out without difficulty. I must confess that I failed to see them, until an Indian pointed out to me, away off on the hill-side, two mere specks moving towards our camp. And what was more remarkable, they had, by a single shout, in that rarefied, electrical atmosphere, conveyed the intelligence that they had found the enemy, and that work was to be done. (Pettis 1878: 13–14)

After a hurried supper, Carson led his men out on a night march. The cavalry and artillery rode ahead, with the infantry staying with the wagon train and given precise instructions about where to rendezvous. During the night march no one was allowed to smoke or speak except for essential orders, which had to be given in a whisper. The cavalry got to the Canadian River valley around midnight and found the trail of a large group of natives. At this point they stopped to wait for daylight, standing silent beside their mounts until dawn.

Kiowa-Apache and Carson's column at First Adobe Walls, November 25, 1864

MAP KEY

1 0700hrs: As dawn breaks, Colonel Christopher "Kit" Carson orders his men to move out of their night camp, where they have been standing in silence holding their horses for hours.

2 0800hrs: After marching 4–5 miles the column is spotted by Kiowa-Apache watering their horses on the opposite bank of the Canadian River. Carson sends some of his cavalry to give chase, and the scouts also join in, but the Kiowa-Apache get away to warn their village.

3 0830hrs: The artillery battery catches up to the lead cavalry and scouts 2 miles west of the Kiowa-Apache village of Chief Dohasan, where they are stealing the village's horses that had been pastured there.

4 0845hrs: The advance cavalry and scouts attack Dohasan's village.

5 0900hrs: The reserve party and artillery make it to the village to find the advance party and scouts have cleared it after a brief skirmish. Chief Dohasan rides off to warn the Comanche villages nearby. The advance party and scouts have moved on toward Adobe Walls, harassing the Kiowa-Apache as they make a fighting retreat.

6 0900–1000hrs: The advance party and scouts fight the Kiowa-Apache all the way to Adobe Walls, and are joined piecemeal by other elements of the command, with the artillery arriving last. The Kiowa-Apache stiffen their resistance and the advance halts at Adobe Walls.

7 1000hrs: The first shots of the artillery from Cannon Hill force the Kiowa-Apache to withdraw. Carson orders his men to water their horses and rest.

8 1215hrs: The Kiowa-Apache return to attack again.

9 1215–1530hrs: The Kiowa-Apache exchange fire with the soldiers as more warriors swell their ranks.

10 1530hrs: Carson, seeing he is outnumbered and spotting a large force of Comanche approaching his position, orders his men to withdraw.

11 1530–1630hrs: The warriors, guessing that the soldiers were headed back to the village, attack the retreating column fiercely, burning the grass around them. Once the soldiers make it to about 500yd east of the village, the warriors hurry to the village to clear out their property.

12 1630hrs: The artillery quickly clears the village of warriors and Carson orders everything burned. The Kiowa-Apache keep their distance. At 1730hrs, sunset ends the battle. The Kiowa-Apache make a final withdrawal and the soldiers finish burning the village.

13 1800–2100hrs: Shortly after sunset, Carson orders his men to move west to find Lieutenant Colonel F.P. Abreu, commanding the infantry and wagon train, and finally reunites with Abreu's force.

Battlefield environment

The Texas Panhandle was open, undulating plains cut by rivers that sank 50–100ft below the surface. These river valleys tended to be broad, sometimes a mile or more, and the river bottom was thick with cane grass growing 6–8ft high even in winter. On the bluffs and plains the grass stood only a couple of feet high, but still high enough to partially conceal a prone man. The winters were cold and windy. During the night of November 24/25, Carson's men had to stand beside their horses for several hours without fires, smoking, or even much movement beyond the spot on which they were rooted. This must have been torturous. The Kiowa-Apache, on the other hand, spent a cozy night in their tepees and enjoyed a hot meal in the morning.

The terrain at Adobe Walls was undulating and open, with much greater visibility than at the river bottom. It was a perfect setting for the artillery. Once at Adobe Walls itself, both sides would be able to see a long distance. The old trading post's walls still stood higher than a man and offered decent protection from gunfire. It was a highly visible landmark, standing as it did on a slight rise and being the only permanent manmade structure for miles. In this Carson was fortunate, because he could see the large number of Kiowa-Apache and Comanche reinforcements approaching and thus knew it was time to withdraw.

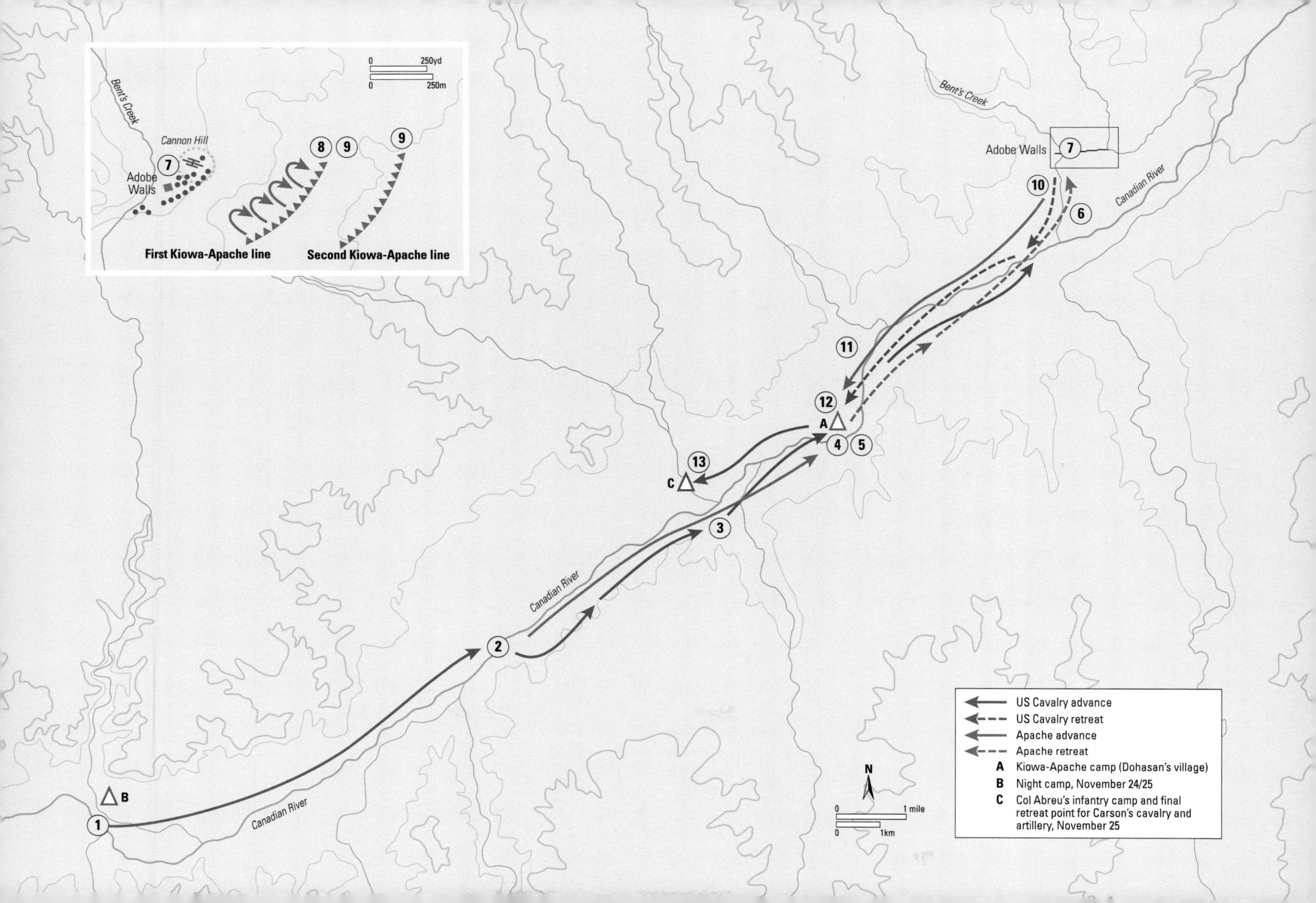

Bent's Creek
Cannon Hill
Adobe Walls
First Kiowa-Apache line
Second Kiowa-Apache line
0 250yd
0 250m
Adobe Walls
Canadian River
Canadian River
Canadian River
US Cavalry advance
US Cavalry retreat
Apache advance
Apache retreat
A Kiowa-Apache camp (Dohasan's village)
B Night camp, November 24/25
C Col Abreu's infantry camp and final retreat point for Carson's cavalry and artillery, November 25
N
0 1 mile
0 1km

INTO COMBAT

At daybreak on November 25 the soldiers broke camp. Carson rode in front with his scouts. Half the cavalry came next, then the infantry and wagons, with the other half of the cavalry bringing up the rear. They were on the north side of the river, and soon heard someone shouting from the south side, "*¡Ven aquí! ¡Ven aquí!*" ("Come here! Come here!"). It was three young Kiowa-Apache out collecting horses. The men had apparently mistaken the column as a group of *comancheros*. Carson sent a company under Major William McCleave, 1st California Cavalry, across the shallow river after them but the trio got away, hurrying back to the camp to sound the alarm. With the element of surprise lost, the scouts swung into action. As scattered shots sounded from across the river, Carson urged his men forward, eager to hit the camp before it became fully aware of the danger. The bulk of the cavalry followed the initial detachment and the scouts across the river, while Carson led the rest along with the cavalry. The men manning the howitzers were on foot and maintained an impressive speed while navigating the howitzers through the tall grass.

McCleave's force hit the Kiowa-Apache camp first. This was the westernmost camp, being about 4 miles west of Adobe Walls. It was the camp of Chief Dohasan ("Little Mountain"), the elderly head chief of the Kiowa-Apache, and was soon abandoned as the Indians fled, the women and children heading for the river bluffs to the north while the men covered their retreat. Once the noncombatants were safe, the Apache-Kiowa warriors kept up a fighting retreat, falling back to the east until they made it to Adobe Walls, where they appear to have been reinforced and their line stiffened. The Kiowa-Apache made several charges, prompting McCleave to order his men to dismount. McCleave corralled his horses within the half-ruined trading post and spread out his men in a skirmish line. It was here that Carson and the rest of the force caught up with the battle. Carson turned to Pettis as soon as he came up and said, "Pettis, throw a few shell into that crowd over thar" (quoted in Pettis 1878: 22). The artillery officer obliged.

> It was now near ten o'clock in the morning, the sky was not obscured by a single cloud, and the sun was shining in all its brightness. Within a hundred yards of the corralled horses in the Adobe Walls, was a small symmetrical conical hill of twenty-five or thirty feet elevation, while in all directions extended a level plain. Carson, McCleave, and a few other officers, occupied the summit, when the battery arrived and took position nearly on the top. Our cavalry was dismounted and deployed as skirmishers in advance, lying in tall grass, and firing an occasional shot at the enemy. Our Indians, mounted and covered with paint and feathers, were charging backwards and forwards and shouting their war cry, and in their front were about two hundred Comanches and Kiowas, equipped as they themselves were, charging in the same manner, with their bodies thrown over the sides of their horses, at a full run, and shooting occasionally under their horses' necks, while the main body of the enemy, numbering twelve or fourteen hundred, with a dozen or more chiefs riding up and down their line haranguing them, seemed to be preparing for a desperate charge on our forces. [Assistant] Surgeon [George S.] Courtright had prepared a corner of the Adobe Walls for a hospital, and was busy, with his assistants, in attending to the wants of half a dozen or more wounded. Fortunately, the Adobe Walls were high enough to protect all our horses from the enemy's rifles, and afford ample protection to our wounded. (Pettis 1878: 23–24)

An unnamed Union cavalry officer, photographed in 1863. His regulation gear is far more suited for fighting in the Eastern Theater than in the Desert Southwest. The regulation kepi gave scant protection from the sun and soldiers out West generally bought their own wide-brimmed hat. The saber was also being phased out at this time because it saw little use in the Apache Wars, although they appear to have been carried during the First Battle of Adobe Walls because the Plains Indians were more likely to close. The red sash would have also been discarded as a useless impediment. The gloves would have been discarded as being too hot, but the men would have been stuck with the hot and itchy wool uniform, which they constantly complained about. The knee boots would have proved useful for protecting the rider's legs from thorns and sharp rocks, although they would have rarely had the nice shine shown here. (Photo by Timothy H. O'Sullivan/Archive Photos/ Getty Images)

When the first howitzer fired, it had an instant effect on the Kiowa-Apache. They rose up in their stirrups, wheeled their horses about, and galloped away. The howitzers fired three more shots, but by the fourth shot the Indians were already out of range. Meanwhile, Dohasan was galloping toward the other Kiowa-Apache and Comanche camps nearby to get reinforcements. In full view of Adobe Wells and about a mile distant east from it stood a Comanche village of more than 500 lodges. Every lodge generally had at least one warrior, and almost always two, so the New Mexico column was facing a considerable force. Carson, however, did not appear to have seen the danger, perhaps thinking the artillery had scared them off for good. He tarried at Adobe Walls, watering his horses and allowing his men to eat for the first time since before their long night march.

The break didn't last long. Soon Dohasan returned with a large force of Comanche and Kiowa-Apache. In his official report, Carson stated, "In a short time I found myself surrounded by at least 1,000 Indian warriors, mounted on first-class horses … They repeatedly charged my command from different points, but were invariably repulsed with great loss" (quoted in Dunlay 2000: 332). Knowing they faced artillery, the warriors dispersed so as to make themselves less of a target. The Indians made an impressive spectacle as they rode back and forth about 200yd from the soldiers' position, firing from beneath the necks of their mounts. Others dismounted, lay prone in the grass, and sniped at the soldiers. Pettis admits they "made it hot for most of us by their excellent marksmanship" (Pettis 1878: 28). This combined attack had a purpose – the Indians were hoping their display of bravery, plus the losses

The second Kiowa-Apache attack

After first being scared off by the artillery fire, which most had never experienced before, the Kiowa-Apache soon regrouped and realized they needed to attack in more open order. The boldest rode back and forth in front of the soldiers, hanging alongside their horses and firing from beneath their necks. This was more a means for eroding the soldiers' morale than for effect. Deadlier were the Kiowa-Apache who had crawled through the grass to get in close and snipe at the soldiers. The soldiers, in turn, lay spaced out between Adobe Walls and Cannon Hill, firing at whomever they could see. They knew that if they broke, the horsemen would ride in for the kill, so as frightened as they may have been, they held their ground.

The Kiowa-Apache and Comanche had a large number of firearms, but they were mostly older models. Many would have been flintlocks, flint being readily available and easy to convert into a striker for a gun. They couldn't make percussion caps, so many Indians preferred older guns. Reports also state a large number of warriors at the battle used bows and arrows. The Kiowa-Apache snipers made poorer targets than the soldiers because after firing a shot or two, they could move to another spot, while Carson's skirmish line had to maintain position. While both sides would reveal themselves with their gun smoke, the tall grass made individuals hard to spot. On the other hand, the horsemen made good targets.

inflicted on the enemy by their snipers in the grass, would cause the soldiers' line to break. Then the riders could swoop in and finish them off.

The fight lasted until late in the afternoon as casualties mounted on both sides. Someone on the Indian side had a bugle and knew the cavalry bugle commands. Every time the cavalry bugler sounded a command, he would sound the opposite one. Apache tradition says this mysterious bugler was Satanta ("White Bear"), one of their chiefs and Dohasan's second-in-command. The Apache say this demoralized and confused the cavalry, while Pettis says the men laughed it off.

As the afternoon wore on, more and more Indian reinforcements arrived from nearby villages. Carson's situation was perilous, and he feared not only that he might be overwhelmed, but that the village he had passed would be packed up and removed before he could destroy it. He admits in his official report that he had "serious doubts for the safety of my rear" (quoted in Dunlay 2000: 334). Trying to salvage what he could of the situation, he decided to withdraw to that village and burn whatever was there. The officers objected:

> The most of our officers were anxious to press on and capture the village immediately in our front, and Carson was at one time about to give orders to that effect, when our Indians prevailed upon him to return and completely destroy the village that we had already captured, and after finding our supply train, replenishing our

A Colt Model 1860 revolver. A large number of these weapons were left over from the Civil War and served in the Indian Wars for many years. The Colt was a well-balanced, accurate gun with good stopping power and a vast improvement over the single-shot Dragoon pistol in terms of rate of fire. Although the cylinder had the capacity for six shots, it was generally only loaded with five, the hammer resting on the empty chamber. If the hammer rested on a charged chamber, there was a good chance of it going off if struck. The pistol was slow to reload and could not easily be done so on horseback, so many men carried extra, preloaded cylinders that could be quickly snapped into place during battle. It was not a perfect weapon for desert fighting, however. The gritty conditions of the Desert Southwest meant that it had to be constantly cleaned and oiled – a wearisome task at the end of a long day's ride in the sun. Proper maintenance was essential to avoid misfires. (NRA Museums, NRAmuseums.com)

> ammunition, and leaving our wounded, we could come back again and finish this village to our satisfaction. After some hesitation and against the wishes of most of his officers, at about half-past three Carson gave orders to bring out the cavalry horses, and formed a column of fours, the number four man of each set of fours to lead the other three horses, with the mountain howitzers to bring up the rear of the column. The balance of the command was thrown out as skirmishers on the front, rear and on both flanks, and we commenced our return march. (Pettis 1878: 31)

Chief Kicking Bird, leader of a peace faction within the Kiowa nation, *c.*1869–74. The Kiowa-Apache were related to but distinct from the Kiowa. They were essentially Apache who had migrated to the Great Plains of the Texas Panhandle and Oklahoma and had taken on many Plains Indian characteristics such as buffalo hunting, tepees, and Plains religion in order to adapt to their new environment. They were a small group and attached themselves to the powerful Kiowa for protection. While they acted as a band of that tribe, they retained their Athabascan (Apachean) language and sense of identity. The Kiowa and Kiowa-Apache rarely intermarried or even learned each other's language, relying on the famous Plains Indian sign language to communicate. (Photo by Authenticated News/Archive Photos/Getty Images)

Returning to the village was no easy matter. The Indians, fanning out on all sides, set the dry grass on fire. This forced the cavalrymen up into the river bluffs, but even there smoke still swirled all around them. The Indians used this as cover for their charges, firing and retreating before the cavalrymen could respond. One got so close he was able to lance a California trooper. A New Mexico soldier also had a close shave, but managed to shoot his opponent and scalp him. Pettis relates that the New Mexican had been bitten by a rattlesnake earlier and had been treated by the surgeon with a shot of whiskey. Perhaps emboldened by this, he went back to fighting:

> His company was now on our left flank, and after we had completed about a mile of our return march, a Comanche rode up to us in a cloud of smoke, when a sudden gust of wind left him completely exposed within twenty feet of the boy who had been bitten by the snake. They both, at the same moment, brought their rifles to their cheeks. The Indian fired a second before the other, and missed his mark, the boy immediately returned the fire, hit his enemy in some vital part (he instantly fell from off his horse) and rushed forward to secure his scalp ... This boy took the only scalp that our party secured during the whole day's fight. (Pettis 1878: 32–33)

The howitzers, despite being on the move, managed to land three rounds in the midst of the pursuing Indians. The column got back to the village just before sundown to find about 30–40 Kiowa-Apache warriors still clearing it out. A few rounds from the howitzers and a determined charge sent them running. A small sand hill about 20ft high near the village was turned into an earthworks and the artillery was set up there to deal with any counterattack. Carson ordered everything destroyed. Two Ute women who had accompanied the Indian scouts found two old, blind Kiowa-Apache as well as two disabled tribespeople. They set upon them with axes and cleaved their heads in. Pettis takes pains to state that none of the cavalrymen knew of this until after it was over.

Among the tepees the cavalrymen found several items of white civilian clothing, an Army ambulance, and a government wagon. Unknown to them, the Kiowa-Apache had several white captives – women and children – who had been spirited away at the first sound of gunfire. By now the sun had set. Carson didn't dare risk staying in the vicinity overnight and ordered his men to mount up. The severely wounded were placed on the gun carriages and two ammunition carts. Within three hours they came upon the infantry guarding the supply wagons, who had been following the cavalry by forced marches. They sat down together and gratefully ate a full meal. Their 30-hour ordeal was over.

The next day they beat a hasty retreat. The Indians dogged the column for a time, the outriders on both sides exchanging a few shots, but there was no attempt at an attack. The cavalry's Indian scouts bought the scalp the

The .52-caliber Sharps carbine. This accurate weapon with its fast rate of fire was popular with the men, although it was not without its limitations. Its paper or linen cartridges could often be spoiled in the harsh environment, which led to their replacement with metallic cartridges in the late 1860s. Also, many guns were Civil War-era surplus and not in the best condition when they made it to the Far West. Early models came with the Lawrence Pellet Primer System, a tube that held a stack of percussion caps and flipped one onto the nipple each time the trigger was pulled and the hammer fell. While this theoretically sped up the rate of fire and made it possible to fire from horseback (when putting a cap on the nipple would be difficult), in practice it wasn't reliable and the device was discontinued in 1863. (NRA Museums, NRAmuseums.com)

New Mexican soldier had taken and replaced their war dance of the march out with a scalp dance on the return march to Fort Bascom – much to the dismay of the soldiers trying to sleep.

It is an open question as to who won at Adobe Walls. Carson had driven into the heart of Comanche and Kiowa-Apache territory, held off repeated attacks from a larger foe, and partially destroyed one of their villages. On the other hand, he had been driven from the field and couldn't attack the remaining villages, probably knowing from his long experience of fighting Indians that they would have scattered by this point. Carson reported he lost two men killed and ten wounded, plus one Jicarilla Apache scout killed and five wounded. Pettis gives the losses as two killed, 21 wounded, with two or three later dying of their wounds. Carson claimed the Indians lost 60 killed and wounded. Pettis says he later spoke with *comancheros* who were in the camp who said the casualties on the Indian side were much higher – 100 killed and 100–150 wounded. The Kiowa-Apache said they lost only five warriors, presumably not counting the Comanche, but given they bore the brunt of the initial fighting their losses must have been higher than that. A friend of Carson's, George Bent, later said:

> Kit Carson told me in 1868, three weeks before he died, that the Indians whipped him in this fight. What saved him was Adobe Fort. When the Indians attacked him he ran back to the old fort to make his stand. Buckskin Charley, the Ute chief, was with Carson in this fight. He says the Kiowas, Comanches and Apaches had Carson whipped. He told me they had to fight fire to keep from being burned up. I bought a race horse from Carson in 1868, the horse he rode during the fight. The Indians followed Carson two or three days after leaving Adobe Fort. This horse I bought had white spots on each side of his back. Carson told me he had the saddle on the horse four days during this fight, and when he took the saddle off the skin came with it. (Quoted in Dunlay 2000: 336)

Any rider knows not to leave a saddle on a horse that long, so Carson must have felt he might have to gallop away at any time. Bent also said the Apache related to the *comancheros* that if it weren't for the "guns that shot twice" (i.e. the artillery), they would never have let a single cavalryman escape.

Cibecue Creek

August 30, 1881

BACKGROUND TO BATTLE

On August 30, 1881, there occurred a battle unique in the Apache Wars, in that it pitted soldiers against not only renegade Apache, but also their own Apache scouts. It was the only instance of a mass uprising of Apache scouts in the history of the service. While the battle was unusual in one way, it was quite ordinary in how it got started – through the actions and attitudes of a few individuals. The onset and fallout from this battle say as much about white–Apache relations as they do about their relative fighting styles.

In 1874, the Cibecue Apache bands, along with their cousins the Chiricahua, were interned at the San Carlos Reservation. The Cibecue were unhappy there and got permission to return to their traditional lands just outside the

White Mountain Apache Das-Luca, Skro-Kit, and Shus-El-Day, who worked as government scouts, in a photograph taken in 1885. They have dressed up for the photo, with American-style clothing showing Apache touches such as feather pendants, breechclouts, and moccasins. Two of the men wear what appear to be medals. These were often given in honor of a treaty with the US Government, although it is unusual for them to be wearing so many. All this finery would be set aside for the march, although the Springfield carbines would of course be retained. (LoC)

Apache warriors ready for battle, 1873. This image has several interesting elements. The man in the center wears a war bonnet. That and the shirt would be set aside for battle, the war bonnet being used more for dances. The man on the left carries a lance with a forged iron head, perhaps purchased or taken in Mexico. The Apache became adept at throwing lances through the childhood game of *mushka*, in which a hoop is thrown and the children have to throw a lance through it. On his hip is a knife in a sheath. The two men both have ammunition belts, perhaps to show us that while the photographer wanted them pictured with traditional weapons, they also owned guns, these being a status symbol among the Apache. (LoC)

reservation. By 1880, most had done so, clustering around Cibecue Creek where there was plentiful water and good farmland. Matters might have been settled if it were not for a medicine man named Noch-ay-det-klinne, who in 1871 had been sent as a peace delegate to visit President Ulysses S. Grant in Washington, DC. The following year he became an Apache scout. A few years later he spent some time in a school in Santa Fe, learning about Christianity. This schooling apparently didn't impress him because soon he was back among his people acting as a medicine man.

Noch-ay-det-klinne came to the attention of government authorities in the summer of 1881 when he announced he could raise the dead, and would raise some of the chiefs who had been killed fighting the whites. He held long ritual dances that attracted large crowds, including some of the Apache scouts. Concern soon grew to fear when Army officials heard that Noch-ay-det-klinne had predicted a time when there would be no more white people in the land. Apache scouts returning from the dances often came back late and were reticent about what they had seen.

Agent Joseph C. Tiffany at the San Carlos Reservation and Brevet Major General Eugene Asa Carr at Fort Apache both invited Noch-ay-det-klinne to come explain himself, but their messages went unanswered. With the dances continuing, something had to be done. On August 15, Tiffany telegraphed to Carr that the medicine man had to be "arrested or killed or both" (quoted in Collins 1999: 24).

Two weeks later, Carr left Fort Apache with five officers, 79 enlisted men of Company D and Company E, 6th Cavalry, and 23 Apache scouts, in order to bring Noch-ay-det-klinne in for questioning. He also took along nine civilians, including packers, a guide, and an interpreter. The scouts were not told the purpose of the march, although they soon suspected.

The mounted column rode for the first day westward unopposed toward Cibecue. That evening at camp, Carr gave the scouts their weapons and 20 rounds. According to Apache reports, he told them of the mission and asked if they were going to use the guns against the soldiers or not. First Sergeant Mose, head of Company A, Apache Scouts, offered to go ahead to talk with the medicine man and reassure him the column had no hostile intent. Carr agreed and Mose and another scout left the next morning.

The scouts, led by Second Lieutenant Thomas Cruse and a guide named John Byrnes, went ahead of the main column. When they got to a point about 1.5 miles from Cibecue Creek and 3 miles from the medicine man's village, they came to a fork in the trail. Both ended up at the village. The scouts

Personnel of the 6th Cavalry pictured somewhere in Arizona, 1880. The men are lined up for roll call and inspection and appear just about to move out onto the trail. Note the bedrolls, indicating that this is a long scout, and also the varied gear. The hats, especially, show a great deal of variation, with some looking almost new and others seriously battered. Not all are regulation, either. The men often added to their kit with their own private purchases, and good officers learned not to complain of this as long as the men were comfortable and able to discharge their duties. Only the officer in the front appears to carry a saber. This weapon had long since been discarded now that the men had repeating rifles. (National Archives)

suggested the Verde Trail, which was longer but stayed close to the creek. Cruse agreed and they continued on this for some time before being recalled by Carr once he made it to the fork. He wanted to go by the shorter trail. The scouts exhibited a great deal of anger for having to turn back, and many soldiers later felt this was because they had already set up an ambush on Cibecue Creek.

As the column went up the shorter route, Apache began to appear in twos and threes from the direction of the creek. Most headed toward the village. The next suspicious event was when an Apache named Sanchez appeared in front of the column and said he was headed home. He then rode down the length of the column toward the creek, apparently counting the men. That was the wrong direction for him to get home.

At 1500hrs the column arrived in the medicine man's village, a small mesa overlooking the creek. The soldiers felt unsettled to see a large number of armed Apache in the area. What happened next is open to debate. Carr states that he went into the medicine man's wickiup and told him through an interpreter that he had to go with him. At first Noch-ay-det-klinne demurred, asking to come along in a few days. When Carr insisted, Noch-ay-det-klinne changed tack and claimed he had wanted to come all along but had been treating a patient. Since this patient had been cured just that morning, he could now come with the soldiers.

Carr warned him that if there was a rescue attempt he would be shot. Noch-ay-det-klinne smiled and said there would be no trouble. The officer was further reassured by the lack of hostility in the camp, although he did note there were few young men around. Noch-ay-det-klinne joined the soldiers on the ride east toward Fort Apache. Carr decided, since it was late in the day, to camp on Cibecue Creek near the Verde Crossing about 2 miles east of Noch-ay-det-klinne's village. Carr described the creek as "a small mountain stream, across which you can jump in many places, and step in some; and the brushy bottom does not average one hundred yards in width" (quoted in Collins 1999: 41).

Cibecue-Apache and Carr's column at Cibecue Creek, August 30, 1881

MAP KEY

1 1545hrs: At Verde Crossing, Carr with Company D picks a campsite.

2 1550hrs: Apache begin to gather near the creek close to camp.

3 1555hrs: Apache scouts ask to move camp and move closer to gathering Apache.

4 1600hrs: Firing starts. After the initial volleys, the Apache move down below the brow of the mesa.

5 1605hrs: The Apache withdraw to the creek bottom and high ground south of the creek.

6 1615hrs: First Lieutenant William Stanton's Company E arrives and flanks the Apache in the creek bottom, forcing them to retreat. Stanton and five men form a skirmish line near the western edge of the brush.

7 1620hrs: Noch-ay-det-klinne is shot by two cavalry troopers.

8 1620–1730hrs: Scattered firing continues until sunset brings an end to the fighting.

9 1730–2300hrs: The soldiers bury their dead, eat dinner, destroy what supplies they cannot bring along, and leave for Fort Apache.

Battlefield environment

Cibecue Creek was a narrow creek flanked by thick brush. The banks rose steeply on both sides and offered some cover in the form of greenery and trees. The exact location of the battle has been lost; in many places the banks are quite steep and can rise up to 12ft from the creek bottom and are covered with a few junipers and open grassland. The stream bottom had a thick growth of bushes. The soldiers' campsite was well situated to dominate the local area, being on a small mesa offering a clear view of all approaches. On the other hand, this made it an easy target, especially from the high ground across the stream. Once again the Apache ended up with the better terrain and greater cover. Neither side had much solid cover. The soldiers hid behind packing crates and saddles, neither of which could be relied upon to stop a bullet, and the Apache only had small trees that did not protect their entire bodies. Both sides had to lie prone in order to offer less of a target.

Unlike at Cieneguilla or Adobe Walls, the soldiers weren't fatigued, having undertaken an easy ride of only a few hours' duration. They also knew the area well. As was the case at those battles, however, the cavalry could not rely on immediate reinforcements, whereas the Apache could draw on warriors from all the nearby settlements.

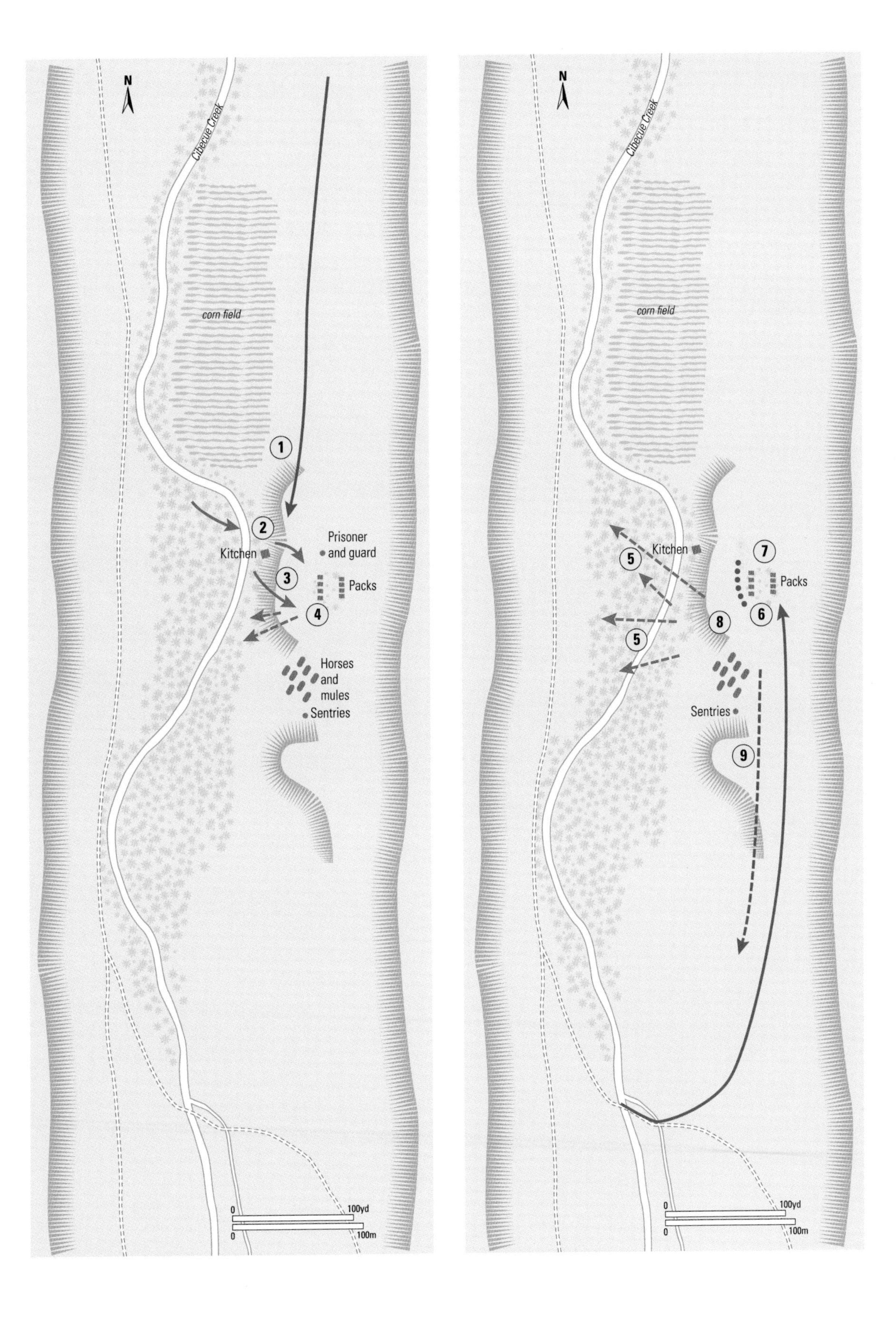
N
Cibecue Creek
corn field
1
2
Kitchen
Prisoner and guard
3
Packs
4
Horses and mules
Sentries
0
100yd
0
100m
N
Cibecue Creek
corn field
Kitchen
5
7
Packs
6
8
5
Sentries
9
0
100yd
0
100m

INTO COMBAT

As the column made camp on a clear and elevated mesa north of the stream, 75–200 armed and mounted Apache began to appear to either side of them. Most were stripped for battle, wearing only a breechclout, moccasins, and a cartridge belt. All but three or four, who had bows, were armed with rifles. Captain Edmund Clarence Hentig, the commander of Company D, called for them to move away but they didn't respond. Hentig noted that an Apache scout named Sergeant Dandy Jim was among them.

Carr told the scouts to camp a little apart from the main camp, as was normal practice. The scouts told Hentig the ground they were assigned had too many ants and they wanted to move. Hentig assented. The scouts then moved closer to the stream bottom and the gathering Apache. While Carr and the other officers felt wary, they did not suspect an attack and ordered the pack train unloaded and supper prepared. Tensions rose as one of the village Apache who was on horseback in the middle of Company D's camp began a loud harangue to his friends. The scouts loaded their .45-70 Springfield rifles. Then the man giving the harangue drew his gun and gave a war cry. A soldier called out "Watch out, they are going to fire" (quoted in Collins 1999: 52).

There were a few shots from the village Apache. A moment later, the Apache scouts let out a volley right into the soldiers, who were caught completely unprepared. They stood scattered about camp, preparing their meals or bedrolls, or taking care of their mounts. That initial volley tore through several soldiers, with those closest to the Apache scouts hit the worst. Carr's adjutant general First Lieutenant W.G.H. Carter, who was one of the closest to the Apache, emerged unscathed and took a shot at a scout named Dandy Bill. Then he bolted for the shelter of Carr's tent 5–6yd away. A warning from another soldier saved his life. Glancing over his shoulder, he saw the scouts about to give another volley and hit the dirt. The bullets whizzed overhead.

The village Apache and scouts then dropped back under the brow of the mesa. Carr called on his men to stand fast. Men got behind saddles or food boxes and started to return fire. The Apache retreated to the creek bottom and the cover of the thick brush there. They immediately got behind bushes or trees and fired back at the camp.

At this point First Lieutenant William Stanton and his Company E, which was a little behind Company D and escorting Noch-ay-det-klinne, arrived at the scene and quickly formed a line. Carr called on them to clear the Apache from the brush but the gunshots drowned out his words. He sent Carter to relay the order and Company E charged the brush, hitting the Apaches in the left flank. This determined attack quickly broke the Apache, who preferred to melt away against strong attacks in order to minimize casualties. Some crossed the creek to a red bluff about 500yd from the campsite. Others took up positions on other spots across the creek. Carr later said Company E "saved the day" (quoted in Collins 1999: 54) with their prompt assault.

Stanton and five men formed a skirmish line near the western edge of the brush on the opposite side of the creek, spacing themselves out so they extended the length of the camp. For a moment there was a lull in the fighting. The Apache repositioned themselves and consulted with each other while the soldiers fortified their position with whatever was at hand – rocks, saddles, *aparejos* (mule packs), and packing crates. Then the Apaches started firing

Troop A, 6th Cavalry are pictured here at a camp on the Mexican border during the Geronimo campaign, 1885. (Arizona Historical Society, #910)

again. Now all of them were engaged and the fire on the exposed camp was so intense Carr ordered his men to lie prone. Few soldiers got the opportunity to fire back.

The deadliest fire came from a hill near the crossing. It was the closest Apache position and level with the mesa on which Company D and Company E were pinned down. The hill had good cover from cedars and brush and all the soldiers could see of their attackers was puffs of smoke from their rifles. Cruse later recalled:

> During the first fifteen minutes of the action, while General Carr was engaged in disposing his troops for defense, he had forgotten his fifteen-year-old son Clarke [Clark], who had come on the march with us. Suddenly he remembered that he had not seen Clarke since the first shot, when the boy was seated on the ground not more than fifty feet from the Scouts. The General's emotion was apparent when he called the boy's name, then turned to the bystanders and asked if they knew where he was. There was an ominous silence for a second, then Clarke answered calmly,
>
> "Here I am! What do you want?"
>
> I think that Clarke was the only person in the whole command who got the slightest degree of enjoyment out of the whole fight. He had a small Winchester .44 and had got to shoot it to his heart's content with none to say "Don't!" (Quoted in Collins 1999: 55)

Carr estimated that only about 60 Apache fired during the initial volleys, but they were soon joined by many more and that for much of the fight the column was exchanging fire with about 200.

Carr had left standing orders to kill Noch-ay-det-klinne if there was an attack or if he tried to escape. When the shooting started, the medicine man and his guard had reached the edge of the camp and dismounted. Noch-ay-det-klinne started crawling for the brush and his Apache friends. Sergeant John F. McDonald spotted the movement and shot him through both thighs even though the sergeant himself had been wounded moments before. The medicine man was still alive, though, and so Trumpeter William Benites shot him in the neck with his pistol.

First Sergeant Mose stayed close to the medicine man and was the only scout who didn't fire upon the soldiers or try to run away. He was nearly shot for his courtesy until Carter called out to the men not to fire on him. Carter turned him over to a soldier, who disarmed and guarded him.

Carr sent out skirmishers to all sides of the camp to protect against any surprise flanking attacks and told his men to hold on. The soldiers, many of whom were veterans of various fights with the Apache, knew this was the best course of action because it was unlikely the Apache would risk high losses by assaulting the mesa. It was more likely that, once they saw they couldn't wipe out the command, they would snipe at the soldiers until nightfall and then leave. This turned out to be exactly what they did.

The fighting continued until nightfall and slackened off as it became dark. After a time it appeared the Apache had left – they rarely attacked at night – and now Carr had to decide his next move. After consulting with his officers, the guide, and chief packer, he decided there was no reason to stay. The survivors buried the dead they could find, ate a hasty cold supper, and packed up all the gear they could on what mounts remained to them. The Apache had taken about half their horses. What supplies they had to leave behind they destroyed.

Before leaving, Carter checked on the body of Noch-ay-det-klinne. Remarkably, he was still alive. Carr feared his miraculous survival would encourage the Apache to fight, so he had Byrnes dispatch the medicine man with an ax.

The US Cavalry had lost seven soldiers killed and two wounded. Most of the casualties had been from the first couple of volleys, when the soldiers were surprised. Three of those killed in action had been watering their horses at the stream and were overrun when the Apache retreated across it. A large number of the casualties were standing only a few yards from the Apache and the bullets passed right through them, causing terrible bleeding. Even if they could have received medical aid, impossible to provide under the circumstances, they would probably have died. The US Cavalry had also lost 42 horses and seven pack mules killed, wounded, or missing.

On the Apache side, the only confirmed casualty was Noch-ay-det-klinne. Some estimates put Apache losses at 18 but there is little solid evidence for this. The Apache themselves said only the medicine man died and several others were wounded.

Carr's column managed to get back to Fort Apache without further attack, but the fight was far from over. The renegade Apache and scouts committed several depredations in the surrounding countryside over the following weeks, resulting in the deaths of dozens of settlers and a few more soldiers. They also attacked Fort Apache in the only attack on a fort in the history of the Apache Wars. On September 1, an unknown number of Apache fired at the fort from long range. The soldiers, fearing a trap, did not come out to fight them but stayed in the fort defending it. Three were injured before night fell and the Apache left.

A view of Fort Apache, January 1884. Founded in 1870, this military base grew in importance due to its proximity to the White Mountain Reservation, which the soldiers at the fort were responsible for guarding. It was the scene of the only Apache attack on a military installation, when it was briefly besieged on September 1, 1881, after the battle of Cibecue. Note the open nature of the fort. Since attacks on large, well-armed settlements were so rare, the Army saw no need to fortify their so-called forts. Soldiers could always barricade themselves in the buildings which the Apache, lacking artillery, would have difficulty attacking. This tactic was used many times by settlers on isolated ranches. Fort Apache continued as an active post until 1924 and is now a historic park. (Photo by PhotoQuest/Getty Images)

On March 3, 1882, three scouts – Dead Shot, Dandy Jim, and Skippy – were found guilty of treason and publicly hanged at Fort Grant. Lieutenant Cruse later stated: "I have always regretted the fate of Deadshot and Skippy. The former was the sage of the Indian company, the latter our clown and wag. I doubted at the time if they had intentional part in the firing upon us. It seemed to me that they were swept into the fight by excitement and the force of evil circumstances" (quoted in Collins 1999: 204). Other soldiers agreed, saying only a few scouts fired on them at first, the rest only joining in when the soldiers started firing indiscriminately at all the Apache.

The Apache account of what happened at Cibecue Creek is quite different, but no one asked their side of the story until Brigadier General George Crook returned to assume command of the Department of Arizona on September 4, 1882. At Fort Apache he interviewed many of the participants. First Sergeant Mose, the lone scout to remain with the soldiers, told him:

> When I took the Doctor [Noch-ay-det-klinne] down to General Carr's camp, I sat down and he set down alongside of me. A soldier came up and began punching the Indian soldiers and telling them to 'ugashe' (go away). Then General Carr's cook began firing at the Indian soldiers; we had hardly reached the camp, when this happened. I was up on the bank with the Doctor. General Carr and Captain Hentig were down in a little ravine close to me, but I couldn't see them. The next thing after that shot was fired, the Indian and the white soldiers began firing at each other. The other Indian soldiers ran into the brush, but I staid [*sic*] where I was. I was sitting alongside the Doctor. The first shot fired at the Doctor didn't hit him; the second wounded him. I laid down behind a pile of aparejos. The Doctor was hit in the head and fell without a word. I got behind the aparejos. That's all I saw. I could hear the Doctor breathing. (Quoted in Collins 1999: 214–15)

Several other Apache repeated the story of the cook firing first, although none gave any reason for it. Some Apache said the soldiers had been acting badly before the cook opened fire. Nodeski said, "When that Captain came out with the soldiers from Fort Apache – General Carr – he let his soldiers turn their horses in upon our corn and it was all destroyed; our cows were killed or stolen, and the same with our mares" (quoted in Collins 1999: 220–21). Crook wrote Major General Irvin McDowell, commander of the Division of the Pacific:

> The Indians are so firmly of the belief that the affair of the Cibeque last year was an attack premeditated by the white soldiers, that I am convinced any attempt to punish one of the Indian soldiers for participation in it would bring on a war.
>
> Without wishing to express an opinion on that affair, I have no doubt from what I know of the Indians and the country in question that, if the Indians had been in earnest, not one of our soldiers could have gotten away from there alive.
>
> Of course, afterwards, it was perfectly natural for the Indians who had lost friends and relations, to commit the depredations, which they did in the vicinity of Fort Apache. (Quoted in Collins 1999: 221)

The battle has become part of Apache folklore, being one of the many tales of suffering from that period. An account by Tom Friday, the son of Dead Shot, was given in 1938:

> On August 30, 1881 my father took fifty scouts and one company of white soldiers to Cibecue to catch a medicine man. This medicine man had been having a big sing and dance at Cibecue every night. He told the Indians that he would bring back all the Indians that had died. Many Indians had a brother dead, or a mother, or a father, or another man friend, and the medicine man told them to dance and he would make them come back alive.
>
> The commanding officer at Fort Apache heard about it that the medicine man made the Indians dance every day and every night. He had him brought into Fort

Apache and warned him not to do that any more. But the medicine man kept right on having dances every night. Then the commanding officer had him arrested again and warned him again.

When the officer heard that they were dancing again he told my father to lead the fifty scouts and one company of White men to the medicine man at Cibecue … the commanding officer called him and said to him, "Dead Shot, take one scout and go over and get that medicine man."

He [the medicine man] was in his camp. They talked to him a long time. They said, "Commanding officer wants to see you."

He said, "No! I no go."

They said, "You see that camp, they will get you. Come with us."

He said, "No, you can't take me. If commanding officer wants me let him come."

They coax him about one half hour then my father said, "Let's go back."

The medicine man said, "Go tell him what I say."

Apache scouts with two of the renegade scouts to be hanged for the Cibecue affair. (Arizona Historical Society, #4593)

My father said, "Commanding officer, medicine man said go yourself. He wants you. You the head man."

Captain Hentig said, "All right, saddle my horse." He took two White soldiers and one scout. He went to the medicine man's camp.

All Cibecue Indian people know that the soldiers were coming. They were ready for them. They were ready to fight. They sent word to all Indians, "Come, clean your guns; get ready."

When Captain Hentig got to camp the scout said, "He is in there." Hentig go right in, just rough like.

The medicine man was all ready, but he don't touch no gun. He just said, "Go out." The commanding officer talked hard. The medicine man said, "Go out." The captain grabbed him right by the top of the hair and took him out of the camp. He got on his horse (the medicine man and one scout on one horse, and two soldiers on the next horse) and they took him back to the soldier's camp. There the captain told them to put handcuffs on the medicine man. Then they put him in a little tent. Then they put a guard in front of the tent, to walk back and forth and back and forth.

All the Indians gathered together and met in a big ditch. The brother of the medicine man was also there. The Indians were all naked. They wore G-strings. They had their guns. The medicine man's brother said, "I will go over there; I will get my brother. No get my brother back, lots of trouble, you shoot." [He then went to the guarded tent where his brother was being held.]

Old "Nana," Apache chief of the Chihenne band (better known as Warm Springs Apache), *c.*1884. Nana had a long career fighting the Americans and Mexicans, starting in the early 1860s or perhaps earlier, and lasting until after most Apache had resigned themselves to life on the reservation. In 1881, at the age of about 80, he led 30 Apache and an equal number of warriors from other tribes on an epic raid, eluding more than 1,000 cavalrymen while fighting eight battles and killing dozens of Americans and Mexicans. He is said to have been killed shortly thereafter by two American civilians, although another report said he moved with his people into captivity and lived until 1896, being about 100 years old at the time of his death. (LoC)

The guard said, "Go back."

The Indian paid no attention to him. He saw his brother in the tent. The commanding officer said to the guard, "Shoot that man." He called the medicine man's brother a very bad name. It made the Indians mad, and before the guard could shoot him he raised his gun to shoot the captain. The guard shot him and the commanding officer went into the camp and shot the medicine man, and then all the Indians started shooting and shot Captain Hentig. Everyone was shooting. About two o'clock the wind blew very hard. The dust blew and the sand blew in big clouds, and you couldn't see much, and everyone was screaming and they ran every way. And the Indians killed the White soldiers' horses, and some horses got scared and ran away. Some soldiers stayed to fight, but many ran away. The Indians all ran at them. Several of the White soldiers and Captain Hentig were killed. None of the Indians were killed but the medicine man and his brother who tried to help him.

The white soldiers started for Fort Apache on foot, that same night. They left their dead behind. The Indians were very angry: they had done no wrong and could not understand why the soldiers would come. So, they went to their [the soldiers'] camp and made a big fire and burned all their bacon and threw the flour and sugar all over the place so they could not use it if they came back.

While all the fighting was going on the Indian scouts, who did not like the way Captain Hentig had dragged the medicine man out by the hair and then called his brother a bad name and then had them both killed, suddenly turned to their own people's side and started shooting at the White soldiers. After the fight they went with the Indians far up the canyons. General Crook sent out word and said, "All the scouts who were in the war come back." He set them all free and did not punish them like the sergeants. The three sergeants did not come back. They were officers and were afraid because of what had happened. They hid out maybe two or three years. Then they thought everyone had forgotten about them, and they came back. They were caught and taken to Fort Grant. There they made a scaffold to hang the three sergeant scouts … All this was told to me afterwards. I was just a small boy when this happened. (Quoted in Collins 1999: 226–28)

It is impossible to reconcile the military and Apache accounts. As with many such situations, the truth will never be known and probably lies somewhere in between.

Analysis

The interactions between settlers and the Apache were always complex, something few settlers but most Apache fully understood. The Apache, with their loose organization under widely scattered bands, never had a unified policy toward the newcomers. Some bands would trade peacefully, while other bands were hostile. The strong individualistic streak in the Apache meant that most bands had mixed reactions to the settlers that changed with the circumstances. This meant that the Apache could never unify against what was obviously a common foe, as many Apache could clearly see. "A common discussion among the Indians of those days was the fact that the Apaches were never able to form a strong confederation, on account of indifference and selfishness on the part of the different chiefs" (Betzinez & Nye 1959: 67–68).

Fighters on both sides showed an ability to adapt to the circumstances. The Apache were quick to improve their weaponry: as early as the Spanish period they were trading for or stealing scrap metal in order to make metal arrowheads, which were superior to those made of flint. Metal arrowheads could be reused while flint often broke on impact. The Apache also saw the advantage of acquiring firearms and discovered which Mexicans and Anglos could be trusted to break their own laws to do so. Despite determined Mexican and American efforts to stamp it out, gunrunning became more efficient with time; so much so that by the 1870s the soldiers were complaining that the Apache warriors they encountered were often as well armed as they were. Captain John Bourke relates an observation of his enemies during a campaign in 1874. "All these [warriors] were armed with Winchester and Springfield breech-loaders, with revolvers and lances whose blades were old cavalry sabres. The little boys carried revolvers, lances, and bows and arrows" (Bourke 1886: 104).

The soldiers, too, had a steep learning curve. The Dragoons came to the Southwest in the 1840s equipped with useless accoutrements such as a shako that was constantly falling off and brass shoulder scales that added unnecessary

"The Apache war – Indian scouts on Geronimo's trail," by Frederic Remington, 1886. Unlike many artists who depicted the Apache Wars for magazines in the eastern United States, Remington was actually familiar with the subject as a result of having spent many years traveling in the American West. His drawings of the soldier's life in barracks and on the trail are some of the most intimate portraits of this period we have. (LoC)

weight and heat. These may have looked snappy on the parade ground, but they were quickly discarded in the field. Their weapons, too, were lacking, and were often replaced with private purchases. Throughout the period we see the men in the field making adaptations long before high command realized they were needed.

Uniforms and equipment for the men improved markedly by the 1860s, but the US Cavalry was hampered by having most of its garrisons stripped away to fight the Civil War. By the time the government began to turn its attention back to the Apache, it found they had taken the opportunity to improve their armaments and establish themselves in strategic locations lost by the settlers during the war. The United States was now fighting an even deadlier enemy than before.

The 1870s saw a gradual improvement for the cavalry, both in terms of their living conditions and equipment, and in the numbers of men they could field; but the real revolution came when the men got Brigadier General George Crook, someone who knew the Apache and knew the land. His innovative use of Apache scouts and mule trains took the fight into the remote mountain strongholds where the Apache had always felt safe. The pressure of numbers that had pushed the Apache out of the lowlands and much of the mountains, was now pressing them in every spot they could go.

Numbers also worked against the Apache in a more subtle way. As they were crowded out of their traditional lands and pushed onto reservations, many began to resign themselves to their new lives. The Apache were encouraged to farm – something they had been doing on a small scale for centuries – but it was still a bitter pill to swallow for the men, whose traditional role was as fighters, leaving the farming to the women and children. Thus when positions as scouts became available, many Apache men jumped at the chance. As one Apache warrior recalled:

> Ours was a race of fighting men – war was our occupation. A rifle was our most cherished possession. And though the scouts were permitted to have only five bullets at a time, and to account for each one fired, a weapon is a weapon. And, believe me, there was not a man who did not envy the scout his rifle. (Ball & Kaywaykla 1970: 170)

Of course, scouts left themselves open to accusations of collusion with the enemy; but the chance to regain their dignity and become warriors again proved to be a strong motivation. Thus, being crowded out by the whites' superior numbers indirectly provided the impetus for Apache to fight against

Apache, and it was this that led to their downfall. Accounts from both sides make it clear that the scouts were instrumental in the final defeat of the Apache. As James Kaywaykla frankly admitted, "It was the scouts whom the Apaches dreaded, for only they knew the trails and the hiding places. And only they could traverse the country rapidly enough to be a menace" (quoted in Ball & Kaywaykla 1970: 197):

Ka-a-te-nay or "Gait-en-eh." Head Chief, Warm Spring Apache, *c.*1884. Part of Victorio's band for a time as well as other groups, he rose to be a leader among his people. He fought especially bitterly against the Apache scouts, whom he perceived as traitors. Relentless in battle, his name means "he who fights without ammunition." Ka-a-te-nay became James Kaywaykla's stepfather, marrying his mother while they were on the run from the cavalry. (LoC)

> Apaches on the warpath, especially when accompanied by women and children, move high up in the mountain ranges whenever they can. This way they can see troops approaching and they avoid many combats by following routes which the soldiers dislike. Troops generally carry their ammunition and supplies by wagon, therefore they follow the flat country. It was only when General George Crook chased the Indians with a column supplied by mule pack trains that the Apaches had a hard time staying out of reach. (Betzinez & Nye 1959: 57)

Captain Bourke recalled Crook's philosophy regarding Apache scouts:

> When prisoners could be induced to enlist as scouts, they should be so enlisted, because the wilder the Apache was, the more he was likely to know of the wiles and stratagems of those still out in the mountains, their hiding-places and intentions. No excuse was to be accepted for leaving a trail; if horses played out, the enemy must be followed on foot, and no sacrifice should be left untried to make the campaign short, sharp, and decisive ... The presence of the Indian scouts saved the white soldiers a great deal of extra fatigue, for the performance of which the Apaches were better qualified. It was one of the fundamental principles upon which General Crook conducted all his operations, to enlist as many of the Indians as could be induced to serve as scouts. (Bourke 1892: 182 & 202)

Aftermath

The attacks at Cibecue Creek and Fort Apache led to a huge response. Several columns of troops converged on the area from surrounding forts, looking for renegade Apache. The hunt culminated on July 17, 1882 in the battle of Big

In 1904, Geronimo attended the World's Fair in St. Louis, albeit under guard, and was especially impressed by the entertainers from around the world and being lifted up in a Ferris wheel. Always quick to see the opportunity in any situation, he took advantage of his celebrity: "I sold my photographs for twenty-five cents, and was allowed to keep ten cents of this for myself. I also wrote my name for ten, fifteen, or twenty-five cents, as the case might be, and kept all of that money. I often made as much as two dollars a day, and when I returned I had plenty of money—more than I had ever owned before" (Geronimo 1971: 197). He never shared his inner thoughts on being part of a living zoo. (Photo by Transcendental Graphics/ Getty Images)

Private William E. Riley, US Cavalry, *c.*1886. Riley wears an 1883-issue slouch hat, an 1884 five-button coat and 1884 gauntlets, dark blue flannel shirt, reinforced cavalry trousers, and high boots. His 1885 web belt holds .45-70 carbine ammunition and the holster holds a Model 1873 Single Action Colt. Riley's armament, equipment, and clothing are a far cry from that of the US Dragoons of the beginning of our period. From head to toe he is much better prepared for campaigning in the rough environment of the Desert Southwest. His slouch hat offered protection from the sun for his head and neck that the laughable Dragoon shako with its tiny front brim did not. The rest of his clothing is more durable and looser than the earlier uniform. He may not have looked as impressive on the parade ground, but there is no evidence the Apache were in any way impressed by snappy uniforms – and white settlers wanted results, not parades. His rifle and sidearm were far superior to the single-shot weapons in use at the beginning of our period, which could not match the rate of fire or even the range of an Apache bow. The evolution of the US Cavalry took several decades, but by the time Riley was serving it could stand toe to toe against the fiercest Apache warriors. Even so, Apache scouts were still required to get the cavalry to the fight. Both sides acknowledge that no amount of improved equipment could have turned the tide without the Apache scouts. (National Archives)

Dry Wash (aka Big Dry Fork), in which troops from several forts caught up with the main renegade band. While the Apache were once again able to escape by fleeing into the woods, 16 Apache, including two mutinous scouts, were killed. After this battle there was little fighting. Those Apache who hadn't been killed or turned themselves in filtered back into their tribes and laid low, or fled to Mexico or the hinterland of the American Southwest.

When Brigadier General Nelson A. Miles took over from Crook on April 11, 1886, he discharged many scouts, deciding to use them only as trackers. He also limited them to only four or five rounds each while on the reservation, for fear they would trade the bullets as currency. While this prohibition created bad feelings, those scouts allowed to stay on continued to serve well.

Miles set up a network of heliograph stations across southeastern Arizona and part of northern Sonora. In pristine conditions, flashes from a heliograph could be seen up to 100 miles away, although 30 miles was a more reliable distance. They used Morse code to send messages at a rate of 5–12 words per

"Naches" (also spelled Naiche) or "Wei-chi-ti," Chiricahua Apache chief and the son of Cochise, is shown here on horseback, March of 1886; Geronimo stands in front of him. Discontented with reservation life, Naiche twice fled with Geronimo to Mexico. After his final capture, he contented himself with painting and became renowned for his depictions of Apache life. He also served as an Apache scout on the reservation in Oklahoma. The last hereditary chief of the Chiricahua band, Naiche died in 1919. (Photo by Time Life Pictures/National Archives/The LIFE Picture Collection/Getty Images)

minute that would be received by an observer equipped with a telescope or binoculars at the next station along the line. In one test, a message was sent from one end of the line to the other, a distance of 400 miles, and the answer came back in four hours. In addition to all these technological advances, Miles had 5,000 soldiers to fight Geronimo's 38 Apache, making it perhaps the most uneven contest in military history, yet still the campaign dragged on for many months.

As Geronimo himself stated, "It is senseless to fight when you cannot hope to win" (Geronimo 1971: 111). In the end it was superior numbers, not better tactics or fighting ability, which defeated the Apache. In the 1840s and 1850s the Apache could hold their own against a small number of settlers and the few cavalry protecting them. They used the American Southwest's vast landscape as a refuge and a tactical advantage. But even in those early days they felt the pinch of reduced territory. A hunting-and-gathering culture needs a large amount of land on which to subsist, so when ranchers and farmers took some of this land it became harder for the Apache to survive. This, in turn, led the warriors to engage in more raiding in order to provide food to their band. Thus the expansion of settlement actually endangered those very same settlements.

The use of Apache scouts was the culmination of the US Cavalry's adaptation to fighting the Apache. In the beginning they made the typical

HARPER'S WEEKLY. 489

ON A HOT TRAIL.—Drawn by T. de Thulstrup.—[See Page 491.]

This print from *Harper's Weekly*, titled "On a Hot Trail," dates to 1885 and shows two scouts tracking hostile Native Americans for Brigadier General Nelson A. Miles, who was campaigning against the Cheyenne at the time. Miles used mostly American frontiersmen in his earlier campaigns and mistrusted the Apache scouts when he was stationed in Arizona. (LoC)

mistake of a "civilized" army fighting an "uncivilized" foe by underestimating their enemy and assuming that regular strategy and tactics would easily defeat them. One would think that the debacle at Cieneguilla would have been a watershed lesson, but it was not to be. Time and again, overconfident soldiers were led into ambushes and found themselves bested by smaller numbers of "savages." A few sharp commanders began to realize they were up against equals, and began to fight accordingly; but the real turning point came when the US Cavalry admitted they couldn't do it alone, and hired Apache to fight Apache. Only then could the final chapter in the Apache Wars be written.

UNIT ORGANIZATIONS

Apache

The Apache lived in bands, which varied in number from a few individuals to a few hundred. As an example, a band numbering 200 would be on the large side. Of the 100 men, 50 would be of fighting age while another 20 would be youths who acted as assistants to the warriors. The other males were small children or the elderly. Of the 100 females, all would be trained to fight as part of their upbringing, although they would be less experienced since they did not go on raiding parties. There were notable exceptions, including the famous female warrior Lozen. When cornered, however, everyone fought.

The Apache fighting unit was a raiding party made up of some of the men from a single band. Sometimes individuals from other bands also joined, and participation was not compulsory for anyone. A typical raiding party might comprise the war chief and 20 warriors, plus five youths acting as assistants and gaining experience to become full warriors.

US Cavalry

The basic cavalry fighting unit was the company, from 1883 called the troop. In 1861, regulations dictated each company have a minimum of, "one captain, one first lieutenant, one second lieutenant, one first sergeant, one company quartermaster-sergeant, four sergeants, eight corporals, two musicians [generally buglers], two farriers, one saddler, one wagoneer, 56 privates: aggregate, 79. Maximum: 72 privates, aggregate, 95."

The company was led by a captain, assisted by two lieutenants, a company first sergeant, a quartermaster sergeant, and a commissary sergeant. The company clerk was usually a sergeant, while the company support clerk was usually a corporal or sergeant. There were two platoons, each led by a lieutenant and consisting in turn of two sections, each led by a sergeant. Each of the eight squads (two per section) was led by a corporal. Some sections had extra corporals; and corporals could also be found filling important roles in company support.

On campaign, actual strength varied due to desertions, illnesses, and casualties, as well as various governmental reorganizations over time. For example, General Orders for May 9, 1877 specified 54 privates per company in the 1st, 6th, and 9th Cavalry; and 84 privates per company in the 2nd, 3rd, 4th, 7th, and 10th Cavalry. All men, of course, could be expected to fight. The unit could be augmented by Apache scouts and civilian mule packers, the latter of whom would fight in an emergency.

Our notional band has three "commanders," but these men were not in charge in a Western sense. One was the chief, who was generally followed because of his intelligence and experience. The war chief was the best leader in combat and only took command when there was fighting to be done. The medicine man was looked to for spiritual guidance and cures. In many bands these roles were conflated into two or, in rare cases, even one person. Many individuals had a particular magic power, such as avoiding snakes, detecting enemies (Lozen was famous for this), or healing. (Photo by Archive Photos/ Getty Images)

BIBLIOGRAPHY

Ball, Eve (1965). "The Apache Scouts: A Chiricahua Appraisal," in *Arizona and the West*, Vol. 7, No. 4 (Winter, 1965): 315–28.

Ball, Eve, & James Kaywaykla (1970). *In the Days of Victorio: Recollections of a Warm Springs Apache.* Tucson, AZ: University of Arizona Press.

Ball, Eve, with Nora Henn & Lynda Sanchez (1980). *Indeh: An Apache Odyssey.* Provo, UT: Brigham Young University Press.

Basso, Keith, editor, from the notes of Grenville Goodwin (1971). *Western Apache Raiding and Warfare.* Tucson, AZ: University of Arizona Press.

Betzinez, Jason, with Wilber Sturtevant Nye (1959). *I Fought with Geronimo.* New York, NY: Stackpole.

Bourke, John (1886). *An Apache Campaign in the Sierra Madre: An Account of the Expedition in Pursuit of the Hostile Chiricahua Apaches in the Spring of 1883.* New York, NY: Charles Scribner's Sons.

Bourke, John (1892). *On the Border with Crook.* New York, NY: Charles Scribner's Sons.

Chamberlain, Kathleen (2007). *Victorio: Apache Warrior and Chief.* Norman, OK: University of Oklahoma Press.

Collins, Charles (1999). *Apache Nightmare: The Battle at Cibecue Creek.* Norman, OK: University of Oklahoma Press.

Crook, George (1946). *General George Crook: His Autobiography.* Norman, OK: University of Oklahoma Press.

Davis, Britton (1972). *The Truth about Geronimo.* Lincoln, NE: Bison Books.

Dunlay, Tom (2000). *Kit Carson & The Indians.* Lincoln, NE: University of Nebraska Press.

Geronimo, ed. S.M. Barrett (1971). *Geronimo: His Own Story.* New York, NY: Ballantine Books.

Gorenfeld, Will (2008). "The Battle of Cieneguilla," in *Wild West Magazine*, February 2008: 38–45.

Gressley, Gene & Henry Porter (1958). "A Soldier with Crook: The Letters of Henry R. Porter," in *Montana: The Magazine of Western History*, Vol. 8, No. 3 (Summer, 1958): 33–47.

Johnson, David, *et al.* (2009). *Final report on the Battle of Cieneguilla: A Jicarilla Apache victory over the U.S. Dragoons, March 30, 1854.* Archaeological Report Series No. 20. Albuquerque, NM: US Dept. of Agriculture, Forest Service, Southwestern Region.

Lynn, Alvin (2014). *Kit Carson and the First Battle of Adobe Walls.* Lubbock, TX: Texas Tech University Press.

McClure, C. Boone, ed. (1948). "The Battle of Adobe Walls, 1864," in *Panhandle-Plains Historical Review*, No. 21: 18–65.

Michnor, Gregory (2003). *Encyclopedia of Indian Wars; Western Battles and Skirmishes, 1850–1890.* Missoula, MT: Mountain Press Publishing.

Moran, George H.R. & E.R. Hagemann (1963). "Arizona Territory-1878: The Diary of George H. R. Moran: Contract Surgeon, United States Army," in *Arizona and the West*, Vol. 5, No. 3 (Autumn, 1963): 249–67.

Pettis, George Henry (1878). *Kit Carson's Fight with the Comanche and Kiowa Indians at the Adobe Walls.* Providence, RI: Rider.

Reedstrom, E. Lisle (1992). *Apache Wars: An Illustrated Battle History.* New York, NY: Sterling Publishing Company, Inc.

Stevens, Robert (1964). "The Apache Menace in Sonora, 1831–1849," in *Arizona and the West*, Vol. 6, No. 3 (Autumn, 1964): 211–22.

Thrapp, Dan (1975). *The Conquest of Apacheria.* Norman, OK: University of Oklahoma Press.

United States War Department (1880–1901). *The War of the Rebellion: A Compilation of the Official Records of the Union and Confederate Armies.* Washington, DC: Government Printing Office.

Utley, Robert (1973). *Frontier Regulars: The United States Army and the Indian, 1866–1891.* New York, NY: Macmillan Publishing Co.

Utley, Robert (1981). *Frontiersmen in Blue: The United States Army and the Indian, 1848–1865.* Lincoln, NE: University of Nebraska Press.

INDEX

References to illustrations are shown in **bold**. References to plates are shown in bold with caption pages in brackets, e.g. **38–39**, (40).